THE FORBIDDEN SECRET OF COPYWRITING

The Underground Secret to Sell Millions and See a Surge of New Customers

DANE KNIGHTON

THE FORBIDDEN SECRET OF COPYWRITING

THE UNDERGROUND SECRET TO SELL MILLIONS AND SEE A SURGE OF NEW CUSTOMERS

© 2019 **DANE KNIGHTON**

ISBN: 978-1-08223-074-5

Category: Business & Money

Cover Design: Desy Suryani

Copy Editor: Lizette Balsdon

Publisher: Dane Knighton Inc

Unit 1-

Level 1

Fulham

London

England

Printed in the United Kingdom

TABLE OF CONTENTS

THE BEGINNINGS

I had just finished one of the worst treatments of my life. Cracks in the corner of my mouth, unable to smile, waking up every day to face the same "uncontrollable" situation I found myself in.

White pillows on the bed covered in patches of blood. Self-confidence hit rock bottom. I couldn't let anyone come near my face and whenever someone looked at me… I "knew" what they were really looking at. Honest-to-God it was eight months of hell. During this time and the past two years, I was diagnosed with a severe condition. It was like having blood blisters all over my face. It sent me into depression, unworthiness and even suicidal thoughts. Insecurity was the norm.

Despite the "state" of my abnormal appearance I still continued to pump out over 770 videos online and over 1,000 pieces of free content. I was determined to make this work. I was working day and night for almost three straight years and still I wasn't able to make more than $20 online. For a long time, I wasn't bothered about making money and publishing fitness content was more of an enjoyable hobby. Until… the time came to make my first "pitch".

Let me tell you something: After this "pitch" I thought I'd made it. I had a feeling of euphoria like no other. I experienced the all mighty… 'make money while you sleep'. I thought to myself "They were right! You can indeed make money in your sleep". The total sales on that day from the first pitch was $7. Now that I've had this euphoric experience nothing was stopping me. Until… I did another "launch" – if you can call it that. Only this time… not one single soul pulled out their wallet.

I was forced to look for answers and wondered why no one was buying my products. You know… I thought as long as the product is great, it kinda sells itself. No wonder my total profit was $0 after refunding my one and only customer. Eventually I came across the secret skill – Copywriting. And that's exactly why I'm writing this book.

Dane Knighton is a marketing consultant and copywriter who works with high level entrepreneurs. He has been watched by over 1.2 million people across the entire globe and they've spent more than 1.5 million minutes watching him speak. As of this writing, Dane is open to occasional speaking engagements. If you would like to book Dane for you speaking engagement go to: **www.daneknightonbook.com/speaking**

INTRODUCTION

W hat you're about to learn is gonna shock you. Once you learn *The Forbidden Secret* that's unseen by the untrained eye, you'll suddenly notice it everywhere.

In this book, I will cover tons of different "techniques" but this secret will be the underlying idea throughout this work. As far as I'm aware, there's no other book exactly like this.

You see, I can tell you all the breakthrough techniques and frameworks to use... however if you don't actually know HOW they're being used against you, and HOW to spot them, then all the information in the world won't help. And that's exactly why I am going to show examples of each technique in action. If one to many selling has always seemed like a maze, I'm about to make it a whole lot simpler. And by the way, it's not your fault that you haven't been told about this *Forbidden Secret*. Many great marketers are raking in millions every day, and they want to keep their cards close to their chests, but I'm about to spill the beans. The curtain is about to open.

Most marketers don't want you to find out these secrets, because once you know them, you'll see them used everywhere. At the end of this book, it's your choice to put some of these secrets into action—or at the very least, when you hire a great copywriter you know what to look for.

By the way, I've used several persuasion secrets in just these few paragraphs. You'll see what I mean in just a little bit. Before we get into the good stuff, I have to say this: Throughout, I will be referring to "he" or "she" so don't be offended. And I won't be making this caveat again. With that said, let's jump straight into it.

THE FORBIDDEN SECRET OF COPYWRITING

W ouldn't you like to know what separates the copywriters that make millions of dollars from the ones that can barely scrape by?

It's just one simple thing. And to be honest with you, I never really understood why it was so important when I first started out. This one thing is *The Forbidden Secret*.

Before I reveal this breakthrough, I must make a confession. A big reason why it works is because of market research. I know; I know… It couldn't get any more boring and tedious than this. But I'm about to change the game for you here. Here's the real reason why research is so critical when it comes to persuasion.

By the way, when I'm referring to persuasion, it's not some woo manipulation thing. It's simply a way to make an argument to get the customer to pull out their wallet and buy the product.

Okay, back to what I was talking about. Whenever you want to persuade someone, you must always start with their model of the world. How many times have you heard someone say they must "convince" this person to buy? Well, every time you try to "convince" someone, it creates resistance.

On the other hand, if you can identify the prospect's model of the world, you can work with him rather than against. You're now swimming with the tide instead of battling against it.

Take this example: I had a dreadful experience in Mexico. On the first night, I was robbed of my phone, wallet, and hotel key. To make matters worse, the hotel food tasted like cardboard and the locals were stubborn as ever. These experiences would lead to a bad perception of Mexico. However, maybe you had a fantastic time. You had great beach parties, met lovely people, and had a great time on the excursions.

We both went to the same location and same hotel, yet our beliefs about Mexico are completely opposite. Due to my past experience, I tell myself a certain story and I come to believe that Mexicans are rude and arrogant. You believe it's a great country with great, friendly people. The prospect's past experiences created their beliefs.

What has this example got to do with copywriting? A lot, actually! I'm about to show you the process of research; but first, I want to highlight the importance of it, so it's not such a dry topic. People cling very tightly to their current beliefs, and without getting the prospect to believe you and the solution, you'll never sell them anything.

So, the real reason why you must nail the research and become an FBI detective, is because you need to enter the conversation going on in the reader's mind. The late Robert Collier popularized this concept, but I don't think many people "get it". The reason why you need to know the target prospect so intimately is because unless you know his feelings, beliefs, desires, there's no way you can get him to buy something.

Here's an analogy to illustrate this point:

Think of a thick metal chain. First, you need to find out where they're currently in their own model of the world. These are the experiences, the stories they tell themselves and the beliefs they've formed. Now from here you can start adding more chain links, one at a time, until you get them to the end to take the desired action. It's crucial that you add one piece at a time. If you add more than one, they won't believe you and they'll be off like a shot.

They must first believe (A), then (B), then (C). Not (A) to (C). Again, it's about the undeniable logical sequence.

Here's how we put all of this in practice:

Start with what the prospect already believes. Let's say for some apparent reason, I was looking for a copywriting client. First, I would start by making a statement about marketing and how it's so important for a business. This is something they already believe (1st agreement). From here on, I start talking about the fact that marketing is an investment and never a cost (2nd agreement). Now, I talk more about the importance of buying customers (3rd agreement).

At this point, I have started with strong talking points that he already agrees with and then slowly start to transition to the end of the chain. From here on, I would talk about the importance of the conversion rate in the marketing funnel and why copy is the number one reason it fails or succeeds (4th agreement). Coming up to the end, I would show him that copywriting is one of the best investments a business owner can make. When he pays me $10,000 for one sales letter and that sales letter makes him $100,000 per month. He has invested $10,000 and got a return of $100,000 per month and still ongoing for months and even years. (5th agreement).

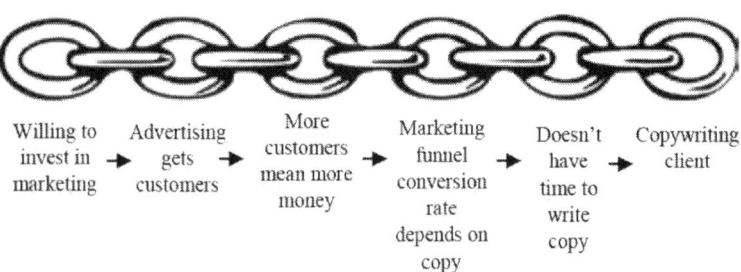

| Willing to invest in marketing | Advertising gets customers | More customers mean more money | Marketing funnel conversion rate depends on copy | Doesn't have time to write copy | Copywriting client |

You see, sometimes outsiders wonder why I'm expensive and can choose who I want to work with. I don't take any shit from clients, especially when it comes to wasting time. I'm the one that dictates and prescribes the solution. After all, they hire me to generate more profit, right?

You know what? Stephen Covey was right! You must "begin with the end in mind". Think back to your younger years:

When you were a child you probably played a game called red-light / green-light or statue. There's basically one person that stands in front (facing forward) and then all the other people start about 30 metres behind him. The person at the front shouts a command and all the other players must try to touch the "commander". If they're caught moving when the leader turns around, they're out.

That's very similar to the point I was making. If you took too many steps at once, you would easily be caught out. However, take one tiny step at a time [strengthen belief] and the leader [prospect] won't be able to detect it. That's just one of the reasons why you should do a thorough job with your research. Throughout the book, you'll see that I'll keep alluding to this point.

You don't start pitching the prospect with the facts that YOU think is right. No! No! It's all about his model of the world. He has had certain experiences and exposures that have led to certain beliefs. Don't attempt to change them from the get-go. It won't work.

Research Your Customers

Ask them about their problems and ask open ended questions. The main job of the research is to really get into the head of your target prospect and identify certain behaviors, beliefs, and feelings around certain topics. Ask them to elaborate on points and see what's important to them. Detect the underlying emotions.

Ask them what problem they are facing and what specific solution they would like. That way you can see what benefits to include into the product and sales letter as well as all the negatives they're experiencing. One of the best tasks you can do as a business owner is interview your current customers. It will tell you so much about their feelings, beliefs, desires, and will give you tons of leverage when you're setting up a new campaign.

When you're speaking to these customers or prospective customers, listen carefully to the words they use. This is so crucial, and here's why:

One of the biggest ways to create trust and rapport is to use the exact same language the prospect uses. This works, because it makes them think that you're exactly like them and shows that you understand how they feel. Throughout the book you'll also see why this is so important.

How do you do this?

Well, you need to get active. As the great Gary Halbert used to say "movement is better than meditation". Go get active and read reviews on Amazon, Reddit, forums, Facebook groups and blog posts, to name a few. Look at what they really enjoy and what they absolutely hate. A good way to do this is using Amazon and going to the books section, then filtering by 1-star and 5-star reviews. The reason this works is because when someone is at either end of the spectrum, they show more emotion. So, when someone gives a 1-star review, they were probably angry and pissed off. That means that they'll pour their hearts out and show the real emotions that you want to tap into.

Again, pay attention to the words they use. These negative reviews are gold. They will provide tons of information especially when it comes to objection handling. For example, let's say someone said they hated the number of stories in the book. That would give you an indicator that the target market that read that book is mainly interested in getting to the point. And that brings us to this point: Look for trends, not just one-offs. If loads of people are complaining about a certain subject and you've seen it on Amazon, Reddit, and Quora (multiple platforms) you know that's something important to note down. I'll say it again. Pay attention to the language and phraseology they use. Because once you get this, you can literally write exactly the way the prospect talks.

Here's the single-most important question you can ask to get to know your market:

"What's important to you about X?"

For example, let's say we're selling a fat loss program:

Q: "What's important to you about losing weight?"

A: "I will like how my body looks".

Q: "What's important to you about how your body looks?"
A: "I feel more confident in my own skin".

Q: "What's important to you about feeling confident in your own skin?"

A: "Well, when I go to the beach with my friends or family, I don't have to be embarrassed anymore when I wear my bikini".

Q: "What's important to you about not being embarrassed?"

A: "It just feels really good. For once in my day, I can be sure of feeling confident. No longer do I have to worry about fitting in my favorite dress. Plus, whenever I take pictures, I don't have to make a certain pose to make me look slimmer. I can **feel** really good about myself.

Just imagine you're writing a sales letter about a product that cures arthritis. You start talking about the daily frustrations the reader experiences. The excruciating pain they suffer when trying to open the jam jar or when twisting a nob on the stove. They will love you for this! They'll feel understood.

Research Your Competitors

I know all this stuff so far may seem dry and boring but stick with me here. Get this wrong and it will cost you millions.

7

Just think about it: If you don't know the person you're writing to and their criteria (values), how on earth can you sell them something? Let's get back to work.

Look at winning ads (**IN YOUR INDUSTRY**). The easiest way to detect these is to look at the ones that have been running for a long time. Sign up to your competitor's newsletters and other marketing methods so that you can see what they're testing and what has worked in the past. Please don't try to re-invent the wheel. It's unnecessary
Don't be afraid of pulling out your wallet. Go through your competitor's sales process. Go look at all their ads and click on them. Pay attention to each step (record your screen or take pictures). Buy their main product and then all the upsells and down sells. After doing this to a few of the closest competitors you'll see certain trends. In fact, it will give you a good idea of the appeal that is currently working. You'll also see what copy is working now. Look at the features and benefits and see which ones would be best to possibly put in the headline.

Look at winning ads (**UNRELATED INDUSTRY**). This will give you some ideas that you could implement in your marketing funnels. As you'll soon see, BIG IDEAS are the corner stone to homerun campaigns. And the best way to get these ideas is usually from unrelated industries.

Research Your Product

One last bit. It's becoming like the Sahara Desert out here isn't it? Pretty dry to me! This point is straight-forward. Buy the product you're writing about, or if it's your own, pretend you've never seen it. Package it up and everything, and start from step 1. When consuming the product, pay close attention to the feelings that the prospect will experience when it's his turn to consume it. How easy is the product? What objections might the prospect have? For example, if it's an electric toy car, an objection of a parent might be "Is this going to scratch my TV?" or something similar.

Questions for The Research Process:

- Who is your customer?

- How old are they typically?

- What attitudes do they have?

- What are their hopes and dreams?

- What are their victories and failures?

- What outside forces do they believe have prevented their best life?

- What are their prejudices?

- What are their core beliefs?

- What existing solutions are available?

- What is the market already using?

- What has their experience been like?

- What does the market like about existing solutions?

- What does the market dislike about existing solutions?

- Are their horror stories about existing solutions?

- Does the market believe the existing solution works? If not, why?

- Has someone tried to solve the market's pain points before in a unique way?

- Is there a controversial story behind why old solutions didn't work?

If you've ever read any marketing books, you'll know that fishing and marketing have many similarities. Here's one of them. Think about this: When a fisherman heads out in the morning to catch some fish, he needs two very important things:

1. Bait
2. Hooks

Now, when the fisherman looks for the piece of bait, does he think of what he likes, or does he think of what will attract the fish he wants? He might want to catch a carp, so he wants to use a worm. Or maybe he wants to catch a different fish, so he'll use a different type of bait. This seems very simple, I know. But the point is that you should spend time thinking like your market (the fish) and you'll do so much better.

THE 3 ESSENTIAL PILLARS

The following few pages are advanced concepts, so hold tight. They're the framework for a winning promotion, so it's essential that I cover them. It's the most advanced portion of this book, so feel free to come back to this chapter numerous times.

If you'd like to know how to tell if a marketing campaign is going to fail out the gates, pay close attention. Eugene Schwartz popularized these two concepts, and it couldn't be more important.

PROSPECT AWARENESS: HOW AWARE IS YOUR PROSPECT?

1. The most aware: Your prospect knows your product, and only needs to know the deal.

2. Product aware: Knows what you sell but not sure if it's right for him.

3. Solution aware: Knows the result he wants, but not that your product provides it.

4. Problem aware: He senses he has a problem but doesn't know there's a solution.

5. Completely unaware: No knowledge of anything, just his own opinion and identity.

Let's look at this picture:

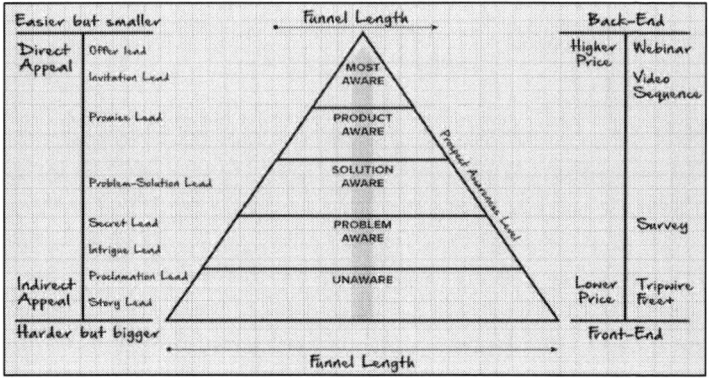

I'm not exactly sure who made this picture, but I got it from Todd Brown. Look at the left side of the picture. You see indirect appeal? Look at the story, proclamation, and secret lead. You have? Good!

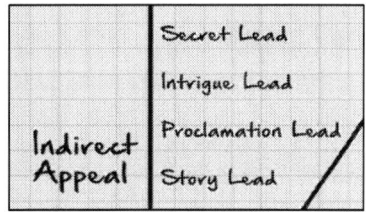

Okay, that all depends on various factors. If you're sending the offer to strangers that have never heard of you, you'll need to start with these indirect leads. Mainly because if you have an "offer lead" and the prospect lands on the sales page and it says "50% OFF", he already knows he is being sold and his guard is up.

Now, look to the right. As you can see, the lower price product will often be sold on the front-end. This is done because the first purchase is always the hardest to get. After that, you've now acquired the customer and can start selling him more products on the back-end without much advertising cost.

Front-end: The main goal of the promotion is to acquire new customers.

Back-end: This is where you sell new products to existing customers.

Two tools that will help you identify the market awareness of the product, include:

1. Google Key Word Tool

2. Google Trends

Here's how to apply these tools in a practical manner: If you've searched for the search term "keto" and you can see that it's on a long upward trend, then you know the market has been exposed to a lot of Keto offers. Not saying that's bad particularly, but it's important to identify these trends for the prospect's awareness. If you go look at all the bestselling Keto offers, there will also probably be some specific trend / appeal. That will show you that the market will most likely begin to fatigue from these certain types of offers, depending on how saturated that specific market is at the time. You'll see in a minute why this is so important as well!

Temperature of Traffic Affects Lead Type

Cold traffic: People have never heard about you before. It generally requires a more INDIRECT lead.
    Why is this and what does it mean, you ask?
Well, consider this for a second: Imagine you see an ad on Facebook and you decide to click on it even though you've never actually consumed any content or info from the guru. Now, imagine you land on the sales page and it says "50% OFF NEW COPYWRITING COURSE", are you going to read the entire sales letter? Or are you going to leave the page in a split second because you didn't expect to be pitched?

Most likely the second one, right? And that's exactly why you need to start off with a very indirect lead. First, you need to grab their attention without setting off their bullshit detector. A story, intrigue, and secret lead would work great!

An example story lead: "There's a new railroad across America... and it's making some people very rich".

To learn more about leads, I recommend (*Great Leads: The 6 easiest ways to start a sales message - By Michael Masterson and John Forde*).

Warm traffic: A problem-solution lead would be a suitable choice here. The prospect most probably trusts you and has consumed some of your content. Your job is to show him the problem he is having and how that is causing him a lot of pain. Then, of course, present the product as the solution. Here the prospect may still be a little turned off by a complete offer lead "50% Off" but may be open to a headline like "New book reveals how to write killer copy and sell up to $5,000 of books per month".

Hot traffic: This one is the easiest. Here you can almost just say that your product is "25% off ". Basically, just telling them the offer is enough. These are your past customers that most likely have also bought multiple products.

I understand all of this "prospect awareness" mumbo jumbo might seem a little tedious, but it can save you millions.
Here's how:
Instead of selling to prospects who are "completely unaware", you now sell to prospects who are problem and solution aware. They already know all the solutions out there, and all you've got to do is sell them on your product.
Unless you have very deep pockets, you can't afford to educate the prospects about their current problem. By the way, it's kind and noble... but just remember nice "guys" finish last. At least that's the case here.

There are different types of prospects on each leaf of the tree, so why not pick the one that is easiest to sell to?

Let me give you an example of this in action. As you may know, my expertise lies in direct response copywriting and consulting with other business owners. I have a few options when it comes to "selling" my service. I can sell to people who:

1. Don't have a clue what copywriting is.

2. Don't know that copy is one of the biggest reasons a marketing funnel succeeds or fails (words are just words in their eyes).

3. Knows what copywriting is and needs better copy.

4. Values great copy and previously hired many copywriters. Spending tons of money on traffic and desperately needs help.

You can figure which one is easiest to sell. Takeaway: Sell to people who are **ALREADY** predisposed to the solution and problem.

UNIQUE MECHANISM

The unique mechanism is the unique ingredient, method, manner, or system that allows your product or service to deliver the desired result. Think of it as the secret weapon your product carries. It is both **new** and **different**. It's the tool that makes your product or service different in how it fulfils on the promise.

Think of the unique mechanism like this:

Imagine a street race like in the movie Fast and Furious where there are four cars lined up at the start. A white, red, green and orange car. The goal of the race is to cross the finish line before the other competitors. Understand this: Each car has a unique element that makes it different.

The Red Dodge has a *supercharger*, the white Nissan Skyline GT-R has a *turbocharger*. The green Ford Escort has *nitrous oxide* and the orange Mazda RX-7 has a *dual exhaust system*. Each of these "modifiers" acts as the **unique mechanism** while the "goal" acts at the **promise**. The goal (promise) is the same for all the cars, yet they have different "tools" (unique mechanisms) to accomplish this.

Let's use the weight loss niche as an example to illustrate the point. We know the main promise in the weight loss niche is to... lose weight. Now let's look at the history and the different types of mechanisms. Rewind about five to eight years ago, and the new craze in this niche was all about eating six meals a day. The mechanism was based on boosting your metabolism and causing faster fat burning. Now, if we go back three to five years ago, it was all about Intermittent fasting and only having a certain period in the day to eat. The mechanism was based on reversing the fat burning process because you're not spiking your insulin levels. The unique mechanism of the Ketogenic diet is "ketosis". Even now, the market is starting to become increasingly saturated, so there are more spin offs from this main mechanism.

All these new diet protocols had their own mechanism and their unique reason why they worked. You've probably heard of Bulletproof coffee, right? Well, there you go - it's a spin off. The keyword is "spin off "; keep that in mind for later. Anyway, you can't make the same boring old promise the market has heard a thousand times. Even though eating fewer calories than your body needs per day is the only way you'll lose body fat, you just can't tell people this. It goes back to ingrained beliefs.

A hundred years ago, you could've made a claim "How to Lose Weight" and people would've bought. Now, the market is becoming increasingly sophisticated which means you need **new** and **different** promises. If you start to look at different industries, you'll constantly see these pivots being made.

The Unique Mechanism offers the prospects a **new** way to get what they've wanted. This gives the prospect hope + belief in themselves... and the new product or opportunity. Because this is something different that they've never tried, it means there are no prior experiences that have led to lifelong beliefs. They're starting with a clean slate.

3 Ways to Create A Unique Mechanism:

1. The Existing Mechanism

Use this when you have a unique piece of the product. It could be a new ingredient, method, or system that no one else has (very rare).

2. The Unspoken Mechanism

The classic Claude Hopkins story serves as a great example. While touring through the Schlitz Brewing facility, Claude Hopkins saw the process used to purify the beer and from then on shared the story. All the beer companies were doing this, but they never spoke about it. Do you have an untold, rare story to tell about the process?

3. The Transubstantiated Mechanism

Turn the ordinary into the extraordinary. Ryan Deiss transubstantiated the low-priced offer into a "trip wire". There should be something new or different with your mechanism. Don't just rename it. Take something that has been done before and either add something or take something away.

Don't sell the generic. Don't sell *How to Get Facebook Leads...* sell your Facebook leads **system**. Don't sell—*How to write a sales letter...* sell your complete copywriting **system**.

Another example: Russell Brunson didn't invent "Funnel Hacking"; he just renamed a very popular NLP technique (modelling) and applied it to marketing. However, he's now associated with it.

MARKET SOPHISTICATION

How many similar products have your prospects already been exposed to before? This is the yin to the yang and a massive reason why so many offers fail right out of the gate.

Let me lay this out for you step-by-step:

Promise:

If your market has not heard about the specific promise before, you just need to make the promise and offer proof— that's it. For example, *"How to lose weight"*.

Promise Explained:

If the market has heard the promise before, and you repeat it, you've lost. Just imagine what would happen if you created an offer that made the promise (*How to lose weight*) and then spent $100,000 on traffic. No matter how great the copy, it would flop. Once they've heard the first few promises about their desired end result (losing weight). You need to bring something different to the table. That means, as a marketer, you must expand the promise while being more specific and believable.

For example: *"Here's How to Lose 30 pounds By Following This 1-Month Plan"*. The promise must be credible and believable. A promise that is smaller and believable is much better than a huge, exaggerated promise that no one believes.

Promise + Unique Mechanism:

Most people should be spending 99% of their time here. That is Promise + Unique Mechanism. You need to ask yourself, which unique piece (that you or your offer brings) makes your product work? - What's in the course that's different? What's in the newsletters that's different? Notice I said **different**. Not just better.

The most overlooked piece in all of this: Knowing what the prospect **already knows**. Here's what I mean: If the prospect already knows how and supposedly why the Keto diet works, because he has already read about it previously. Don't bore him by harping on the same reason why the Keto diet works. He already knows! Are you starting to see why all this is so important?

You can have the best copy, but if you mess this up, it's all a waste. The main reason why the mechanism works is because it prevents mental opt-out. If he has seen similar claims before—and they've failed him in the past - he has zero **belief** in that same mechanism. But, with a unique mechanism, you'll hook him in. It must be different and new.

Promise + Expanded Mechanism:

When other people start using the same mechanism (Keto), you then need to pivot and expand your unique mechanism to new and different items. HINT: Bulletproof Coffee. This product concept wouldn't have sold one product, if it was all about regular coffee and how it helps you burn more fat because of the caffeine and so on.

Dave Asprey told the story and the reason why it's so good for you. The fact that it has yak butter and some other weird oils. This is a perfect example! It's new and different! While we're on this point, another big reason why this grew so fast has a lot to do with the prospect's mental model of the world. Instead of trying to change the prospect's actions altogether, he took something they were already doing daily (drinking coffee) and added a slight twist (Unique Mechanism).

In other words, if the prospect has seen it before, it can seem repetitive, and he won't believe it anymore. By the way, this is forever an ongoing process. Whenever someone creates a new market, over time it will become more saturated and therefore you need to create a new / different mechanism. A popular example is the blue and red ocean theory. The ocean becomes bloody because everyone is making the same claims (market becomes saturated). Eventually, someone creates a new sub section (blue ocean) and opens an entire market, just by providing something new and different. Over time, this new blue ocean will grow into a larger market, and it will become bloody. Again, someone else would need to create something different to create a new fresh blue ocean. The cycle never stops.

Identification—It's all about him:

So, what do you do when the market is saturated, and they no longer believe any promises? For example, if I made the promise: *"How to lose weight using the Keto diet"* people would just glance over it. But... If I said something like this: "Why Haven't **Single Mums Aged 35-45** Been Told About This Diet?". The result would be completely different.

You see what I did there? I called my target market out! I didn't mention anything about the Keto diet (even though I will later be selling them that). To persuade and change the prospect's beliefs, you must start with the facts that she is willing to accept. Gradually you can add more chains to bridge the gap. It must be in relation to the prospect's model of the world. If these single mums didn't believe they could succeed with fat loss on a Keto diet (due to past experiences) they would immediately disregard the pitch when I mention "Keto diet" in the headline. A quick but very important side tangent: Copywriting is essentially more about channeling the prospect's current beliefs or story he is telling himself than talking about benefits. Once you can get him to believe the solution you're offering will get him to the desired result, he will be more willing to buy the product.

Here's why the unique mechanism works:

1. **People have tried previous products and failed many times over.**

If they've tried the Keto diet and failed previously, good luck selling a Keto weight loss product. It's very difficult to sell someone something they have previously failed at. Remember, experiences lead to a belief. So, if someone has done a Keto diet and it didn't work, their belief could be "The Keto diet didn't work because I didn't lose any body fat".

2. They don't want to be told they're wrong.

If you're selling a "similar / samey" product, you're telling them it's their fault. No one wants to admit it's their fault.

3. Sell greener pastures.

Instead of boring old "improvement" offers sell them the latest shiny object. People are always looking for the new magic bullet. Few people are willing to buy similar products just to find one single nugget they can use. Most want the new thing that will solve all their problems.

THE NORTH STAR

The North Start is the Big Idea! Examples of a Big Idea:

"There's a New Railroad Across America and it's Making Some People Very Rich".

"Amazing Secret Discovered by One-Legged Golfer Adds 50 Yards to Your Drives, Eliminates Hooks and Slices… And Can Slash Up to 10 Strokes from Your Game Almost Overnight!"

The Big Idea behind the promotion is the single biggest reason why it will work or fail. To be honest with you, when I first started, I never really understood the concept behind a "Big Idea". It just sounded like some woo woo stuff. Let me explain the importance of it and show you some examples.

What is the difference between these two books? Now that I talking about the topic, you probably already know. You're cheating! Yes! It's the "BIG IDEA" that makes the difference. Listen, the information inside both these books could be very similar. After all, they're both talking about outsourcing business.

The 4-Hour Work Week is selling the desired end result of a lot of people—quit your job and live anywhere in the world, while only working a few hours per week. The other book is selling the actual "thing" (how to outsource). Talk about being dry, hey?

Here are some of the reasons why the Big Idea is so important:

1. The marketplace is crowded, and even worse, there's hype and exaggerated claims.

2. People are bored to death with being bombarded with claims left, right and center.

3. You'll be automatically "categorized"—forgotten—if you don't have one. Your product will just be another piece of garbage in the scrapyard.

Just in case you're not convinced of the necessity and requirement of the Big Idea here's another example. I know I keep promising that the good stuff is about to come really shortly, but stay with me here... I can give you all the tricks and gadgets, but without the solid framework, everything will topple.

What if I told you that you could write 51 pages of words and you will generate up to 600,000 customers and millions of dollars—sounds pretty good, huh?

Take a look at this promotion from Agora Financial. They're one of the biggest direct response companies in the world. Throughout this book, I will use Agora Financial as an example, as they have some wicked copywriters.

They sold the Big Idea—America is about to experience a "currency crisis". They didn't try to sell the financial newsletter by telling readers about the features and benefits. They sold the idea.

There are many companies that are selling "financial newsletters"; not the eight-hundred-pound gorilla, Agora INC. They're always selling Big Ideas.

Here are some elements that make a BIG IDEA:

- ONE Great Idea

- Big Promise + Believable (creates intrigue)

- Unique (has never seen anything like it)

- New and Simple to understand

- Beneficial to the reader

- Specific (adds believability)

The Biggest Reasons Why Your Promotion Will Fail:

1. Big Idea
2. Presentation

Without a Big Idea, your promotion will fail! It needs to be believable, simple, and timely. Timing is huge here! One of the main reasons why that promotion worked, is because of timing. As far as I know, they wrote a promotion almost exactly like that, however it bombed. They waited a while and then published it again, and it took off like a wildfire.

The **Big Idea** is the secret to making an offer work on cold traffic. Plus, high average order value (AOV). Once you get an offer working on cold traffic, you can scale it to the moon and acquire a surge of new customers for "free".

Just before I tell you how to find your Big Idea, let me tell you a quick story. Not too long ago, I was rolling out a fitness offer. I worked day and night to get this offer to work—and preparing a two-hundred slide webinar and everything. I was playing my heart out. The copy on the webinar seemed great and the landing page copy wasn't too bad. Even though I did all this work, I'm guessing you know why my offer failed miserably, right?

If you guessed the Big Idea, you're spot on! I was making a promise that everyone else was making *"how to lose weight"*. Although I did call my market and their current problems out, there wasn't an exciting Big Idea. Essentially, I stumbled to the ATM, grabbed some cash, sprinted home, took a lighter, and set it on fire. Now you can see the importance of the Big Idea.

There Are 2 Primary Ways to Find Your Big Idea

Active Thinking:

- Associations: Use your imagination.

- Opposites: P90x the Fitness Company (Unique Mechanism: Muscle Confusion)—positioned themselves completely against all the other offers. Instead of saying "just follow this diet and these easy exercises and you'll lose weight", they came balls to the wall and said "This isn't easy. It's going to be hard, but you'll get the results you want at the end of the day". They took a position!

- Adding something else: Domino's Pizza added the fast delivery and completely changed the industry.

- Current events and celebrities: This again ties in with timing. In fact, Agora Financial uses this a lot. As far as I know, they are currently running two popular control sales letters. One based on "Trump" and the other based on "Marijuana". These are all recent events—the Trump election and the Marijuana being recently legalized in some states.

- Subtracting: I guess the "takeaway drive through" is a good example of this. It takes less time for the customer to collect the product.

- Find a way to tie random things together: Here you need to use your imagination a bit. Just like I used a metaphor about metal chain links, see if you can tie your offer into something random. Just a word of caution: Be sure to tie it into something the prospect would be familiar with (a very broad topic most people have experienced).

Very Little Thinking (meditative state):

I'm not suggesting that you sit in the corner and wait for an idea to pop into your mind. You'll be there forever. Dust and cobwebs would end up surrounding you. You need to prepare yourself. And how do you do this?

Do a ton of research and gather loads of info (in current industry and other non-related industries). Pretend you brain is like a computer. You just want to download and provide as much input as possible, almost to the point that the PC runs out of storage.

Once you've done all this… That's when you can relax a little and sleep on it a few days. You must cram your unconscious mind first though. This is also why copywriters are usually not paid on an hourly basis, because your mind is constantly working. I'm in the business of exceeding expectations. Here's another unusual method that I heard from Parris Lampropolous. I think he may have gotten it from someone else.

Anyway, it's called the 11th element. Before you go to bed, write to your subconscious. Literally sit down and get a pen and paper and write to your subconscious. Start the letter with "Dear Subconscious" and then write about the things you would like to happen.

I've never done this myself, but apparently this works like gangbusters. Once you've written the letter, have a dedicated place where you put all of them. Maybe this gets you into a certain "state" or something. Who knows? But if it works, that's all we care about.

The word "Big Idea" just seems so daunting. But it's actually very simple. Big Ideas are just two separate ideas that are linked together. For example, let's take "continuity" - the concept of billing someone every month without them having to make a manual payment. I'm not exactly sure which industry started it, but it's now used across many. You can take one idea from one industry and plug it into the next. I know some barbershops use "continuity" so the customer can come as often as they like. By the way, you can only get you hair cut so many times a month. Pretty good marketing tactic!

The point I was making: Ideas aren't these things that come out of nowhere. You brain needs some sort of input. I can't emphasize this enough. Ideas are found in the research.

Just in case I didn't make myself clear…We sell ideas not products. We're in the idea business. Agora doesn't sell the financial newsletter—they sell the idea (Pot Stocks) and the newsletter is just the "fulfilment" piece. (Applicable to Information Publishing).

URGENT: JUNE 13TH DEADLINE APPROACHING!

"WEED-tirement"

You see, all these financial publishers have the same fulfillment piece (newsletter). But they all sell different IDEAS! The example above is selling the idea of pot stocks and you should be investing in them due to the recent legalization of cannabis. The second example (below) is based on the idea that the smartphone is creating a whole new $12.3 trillion industry. Same deliverable, different ideas.

Salesmanship has changed. You can't just corner someone and answer every single objection. Prospects are being smashed with marketing and truthfully, they have tons of choices due to the internet. Before a prospect buys the product, they must first have these feelings:

1. Trust.
2. Same values.
3. Some sort of bond.

You need to make two sales, not one, as most people think. First, you need to sell the prospect on you or the "guru's" values, and when the values between prospect and guru match, it creates a strong bond. This is all about knowing your prospect's criteria, which constitutes their model of the world. Take a group of friends that have just watched a soccer match. Three of them say, "It was an awful game; the referee is a cheating bastard".

The fourth one says, "It was a great game; we only lost by one point and the team made loads of successful passes". They all experienced the same event, but one of them had different criteria. The same goes in copywriting. You need to identify your prospects' criteria (the way they see the world). Once you've established these three values, you're not selling the product for the sake of it. It's much more than that.

"The Day Your Smartphone Made You Stupid Rich"

HEADLINE AND LEAD

N ow we're starting to get to the fun stuff. As we go through the components that make a great sales letter, I'll show you examples throughout so you can see how they're practically applied.

The headline has four main purposes:

One: Draw attention

There are two primary ways to do this: Pattern interrupts, or a straightforward promise. Here's an example of a pattern interrupt:

> ## These Mysterious "M-Boxes" – Hidden in Your Neighborhood – Are About to Spark a $12 Trillion 5G Cash Rush...

The writers jolt you out of your daily life. It's something that you drive past every day, and you've never actually paid attention to it. Plus, it's about to cause a $12 Trillion cash rush. This certainly gets attention. There are two ways you can use pattern interrupts:

1. The words you use—This is (overused) words such as "Attention", "Warning", and similar words.

2. Conceptually—Adding in unrelated ideas (that are still) related to the thing you're selling. The Big Idea (story) is a pattern interrupt (previous example).

In a second, you'll see an example of a straight promise when I talk about the 4 U's.

Two: Select your target audience

Here you can use a person's name (if you can) or in most cases, you can use certain power words and lingo with which the target market can identify. For example:

"Amazing Secret Discovered by One-Legged Golfer **Adds 50 Yards** to Your **Drives**. Eliminates **Hooks** and **Slices**... And Can **Slash Up to 10 Strokes** from Your Game Almost Overnight!"

Can you see the use of these words and phraseology that target the reader? Who else would be using these words except golfers, hey?

Three: Bring them into the full ad

Spark their curiosity on fire so they need to read on to find out more. If you're a golfer, you need to read the rest of that ad. The story creates so much intrigue that the reader wonders "If a one-legged man can do this, why can't I, and how does he do it?"

Four: Deliver a complete message

Communicate to the reader what he is about to learn and how he will benefit from reading this message. The main purpose of the headline is to grab attention and hook the reader. You're not selling anything in the headline. Correction: you're selling the next sentence, and then the next. The headline is aimed at a specific audience and offers the "target market" something they want.

Here's a checklist that I use every time I write or dissect a sales letter. It's not mine personally, but what I got from Bob Bly. Let's look at this example to illustrate these points. Pay close attention here and look how the writer includes all these 4 U's.

Urgent: He applied this by using the word "today". Later in the book, I'll cover the power of urgency and persuasion. If it's not used sparingly, then it will cause some massive issues. Whenever you want to use urgency in the headline, make it more indirect and subtle rather than direct. The word "today" doesn't sound too direct; it subtly implies that the offer will end soon.

Ultra-Specific: He applied this by using specific *numbers* "250". Sometimes you'll see specificity used in *language*, for example "**Tiny** 2.2 Million Dollar Company in **Dallas**, Texas Humiliates Wall Street Experts for the 12th Consecutive Year" —The words "tiny" and "Dallas" imply that you've done extensive research and leads to more believability.

Unique: This all comes down to novelty. Is this new and different or has it been done before? The promotion is selling a Marijuana Millionaire Playbook. That's pretty unique, don't you think?

Useful: Here the writer implies the benefit that the reader could become a millionaire by reading this new marijuana playbook. He doesn't say it outright, but by using the word "Millionaire" it communicates the benefit. As prospects' level of skepticism is increasing, implying benefits would, in most cases, be more effective (depending on the market).

In most cases, the headline should accentuate the positive. Show the after, not the before. For example, if you're a dentist you wouldn't produce an advertisement showing the "bad side". Instead of showing the yellow teeth, you'll show the desired result the reader wants (white teeth). As I've just mentioned, the headline can tell a story and through that stokes curiosity.

It must select the right audience and the product being sold must be relevant.

5 Elements of a Great Headline:

- Self-interest (benefit for the reader).
- News.
- Curiosity.
- Believability.
- Suggest there's a quick and easy way.

Let's see how the writer uses these 5 elements in the promotion:

Self Interest: This is basically the benefit the reader is getting by reading the entire message "Millionaire".

News: "today". In addition to creating urgency, it also adds some news. Oftentimes, people will use words like "Brand New Book Reveals", "Discover" and similar enticing words.

Curiosity: The reader thinks "Marijuana Millionaire Playbook, what the hell is this?" Recently, cannabis was legalized in some states of the United States, so maybe there's something of value here.

Believability: The claim isn't exaggerated and hyped up. The number "250" is also believable. If it said something like "Only 10 copies" it would be far from believable, because the reader has heard it all before.

Suggests there's a quick and easy way: This one is very popular, but there's one thing that you must do. Again, to get maximum believability, you need to communicate this indirectly. If you said "Claim Your Free Book That Will Make You Rich the Fastest and Easiest Way Possible", the reader will know your full of shit. But... the word "Playbook" implies it's already proven, and it's laid out step-by-step. Same with the word "Blueprint"—it communicates roughly the same thing.

As you can see, there's a lot going on. But once you know what to look for, it becomes so much easier. Another thing that is also included in the headline or above, is usually some credibility as well. We will get to that a bit later.

You see, when it comes to writing phenomenal copy, A-level copywriters understand the Core Emotional Complex. They really drill the prospects' emotional hot buttons. They grip that button and rattle it vigorously until those emotions are rattled up inside of them, whereas the lower level copywriters just pile benefit upon benefit. They talk about all the benefits of a greener lawn, rather than talking about the embarrassment the prospect will feel, when all the neighbors have lush green grass and they're the only ones that don't take care of it. They tap into the fear of what other people will think of them, and at the same time, show how powerful and recognized the prospect will be when he has the lush green lawn and all his neighbors and friends are complimenting him.

In other words, to write great leads you must appeal to deep emotions beneath the surface. Scrap the surface-level fluff.

There's one caveat though:

You can't bring these up directly. You must be more indirect and imply or suggest this to the reader. Paint the picture for him. Remember, you don't make the prospect think a certain way. You meet them where they're at emotionally, and you enter the conversation that's going on in their minds. You start with something they can agree with, and then stimulate the existing emotions.

Let me say it again:

Whenever you want to persuade anyone, you first need to start with their model of the world (their own beliefs and feelings) and then slowly but surely take them from the first chain link, to the next chain link. So, on one end is their current beliefs and on the other end, is the belief they need to purchase the product.

PURPOSE OF THE LEAD

Here I will address the topic of "teasing". This might get a little sexual, so get ready (no pun intended).

Whenever you write a lead, you want to tease and then tease some more. Use some goddam foreplay. Unless you're writing to your already existing customers that have bought multiple times, this rule applies almost always. Just imagine, if you had to read a sales page and you don't even know the person... The first thing you see is "25% OFF + [INSERT PRODUCT]". This is dreadful. You haven't built up any anticipation and desire. It's all about the anticipation. I'm no dating professional, but as far as I'm aware, the anticipation of the climax is the best part of the experience. The same goes for selling products. By the way, this will be even more important for front-end offers that are running to cold traffic.

Okay, you might be feeling a little uncomfortable, so let me use another example to illustrate the point. When you buy a book from Amazon, just think about the best part of the process. It's not really the point of purchase or reading the book. It's the time in between when you're waiting for it to be delivered [the anticipation].

What's the use of all this foreplay? It's simple. It gets the prospect committed to reading the rest of the sales message. Without this, the rest of the sales message is a complete waste of time. The structure is also very important: You'll see a very common pattern in "secret leads". The writer will first tease the prospect and only then fully introduce the "guru" and build credibility. When I say "guru", I'm referring to the personality in the sales message.

Here's an example of building intrigue:

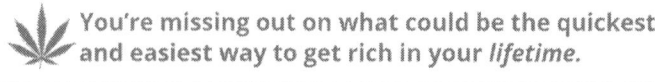

You're missing out on what could be the quickest and easiest way to get rich in your *lifetime*.

Pay attention to the "tease factor". He is using "blind" promises. The words "the quickest and easiest way"—builds intrigue, but it makes you think "what is this?" The fact that it's easy to start and everyone can do it creates even more intrigue, because the result seems more within reach.

Look at the next picture:

> And because many of these marijuana stocks are still trading for just pennies...

It covers an objection (money) while the word "**these**" continues to build intrigue and keeps the reader guessing. Are you getting the point? You don't reveal the solution. You don't go and say—"Pot Stocks is the once in a lifetime boom". You must build anticipation. I mean, c'mon man! Give the prospect some excitement.

Look at this example: The writer has increased the reader's desire and piqued their curiosity. At this point, he wants to find out how to claim his free book and discover details of the offer. But... the writer knows this, and transitions to the credibility section to maintain his attention.

> But first, let me fully introduce myself...
>
> Before I Show You How to Claim Your
> *Marijuana Millionaire Playbook,*
> Let Me Introduce Myself
>
> Credibility Section
>
> As I mentioned earlier, my name is Ray Blanco.

You're still holding tight? Good! Let's crack on. **Here are some elements you can use in your lead:**

- Use quick and easy to read sentences and short words.
- Get "Yes" agreements (start with what they agree with).
- Make statements that are honest and believable.

As I've already established—a great lead:

1. Gets emotional juices flowing.
2. Creates unconscious feelings.

Arouse curiosity, build intrigue, create anticipation, open the reader's mind, build trust, create a bond, and **set up the persuasion that is about to follow**. Read that bold text again. Now, that's what separates the man from the child. The great copywriter is always looking a few steps ahead.

Here are some key terms you should know:

Neologizing—giving a key concept a new name to spark curiosity by creating a NEW, intriguing name. You'll see this all the time in "secret leads" and bullets.

This Tool Is So Powerful...
I Am Calling It the Income Box

This "income box" is just an ordinary subject. The reason it's so powerful is because it stimulates novelty and communicates new. There's one thing in copy that you really don't want to do, and that is, bore the reader by telling him something he already knows. This illustrates again why foreplay is so important. What would happen if you said this in the lead?

"Buy Apple stock now! It's increasing". The prospect will head straight to Google and search "Apple Stock".
    But...If you said "Buy this **"FXX2" stock**—it's currently increasing 25%", —that communicates new! They don't know what "FXX2 stock" is. I just made it up. This also tells the prospect the only place he can get this information is right here, right now. Nowhere else. I'll talk more about the communication of "only" and "new" in a second. By giving an old, boring concept a new name, you keep the reader's attention so he cannot go and...

Google it. At the same time, it also creates more intrigue, and increases perceived value and anticipation.

Transubstantiation: Turn something ordinary into something special. Here's a current example:

Internet marketer Frank Kern is currently running an offer called "Intent Based Branding". Now to be honest with you, I haven't purchased the course, so this isn't going to be 100% accurate, but it will suffice as an example. This is a classic example of turning something ordinary into something special. As far I know, the main concept behind "Intent Based Branding" is simply:

Creating value-based content, re-targeting the viewers that have showed interest (repeatedly), which creates an omnipresence effect. And you do this by trying to get a funnel that breaks-even and therefore acquire customers while at the same time creating a "brand". It's basically a by-product of direct response marketing, but the fact that you can use pixel re-targeting on social media, enables you to follow the audience everywhere.

Of course, there's more to it than this, like the right messaging and stories. If Frank was pitching the product, but didn't transubstantiate a "boring" concept into something new, his sales would definitely be much lower, because the prospects already know what he is selling. Novelty sells.

THE RULE OF ONE

I n most of your marketing, you should never have one of anything. Not one customer, not one media channel, not one merchant account. Not one of anything! This is the rare case.

We're starting to get to some of the principles of persuasion. This is most definitely one of them. If you pay attention to human behavior, you'll be able to identify this for yourself. Whenever humans buy or seek a solution, you'll often hear the words "what's the one thing that I need to do [insert problem]?"

In fact, let me pull up an example to show you the impact of this concept. When you see this, you're going to freak out. Okay, I've just Googled "bestselling business books of all time".

Here are the results:
The Four-Hour Work Week, Good to Great, Crush It, Get over Your Damn Self, Business Model Generation, The Advantage, Winning, The $100 Start Up, Rework, Great by Choice, The Power of Broke.

From here on, in no order, pay attention to the words used:

- The Three Laws of Performance
- The Four Disciplines of Execution
- The Start Up's Owner's Manual
- The Innovator's Dilemma
- The Innovator's Solution
- The Halo Effect

Have you seen the pattern yet? I damn well hope so. If not, they were all based on ONE idea. The word "**The**" explains it all.

I swear there's something about humans where we like to grasp one thing. Just imagine, if *The 4-hour work week* was titled *"Outsource personal assistants from Thailand"* instead. That's not sexy at all.

In a nutshell, you want:

One big simple idea which yanks the heart (engages the emotions) and then also engages the mind. It's easy to understand and believe. This one idea is then…

Supported by stories, predictions, statements, and promises. It's like a dart board. The ONE Big Idea is the bullseye and all the other targets are the ones supporting or holding the bullseye together. And boy, oh boy, once you strike that bullseye with a fresh metal dart, is the prospect gonna be so much closer to buying? You betcha!

One core emotion: Here's an example that 99% of humans can identify with. The headline: "Are You Ever Tongue-Tied at a Party?" The writer has tapped into one powerful core emotion. *Embarrassment*. This has happened to everyone, and it continues to happen every day.

Just think about it: How many times have you seen guys at a party just holding their drinks in a corner and staring at girls all night without talking to them? In fact, they don't even have the balls to socialize with other guys. It shows how strong this emotion really is. The only reason these guys aren't out there talking to women, dancing, having tons of fun, is because they have the fear of embarrassment and potential rejection. This is hardwired into us. Penetrate one core emotion.

One intriguing story: With this example, the reader relates to his own experience and plays back the movie in his mind's eye when he was last in this situation and how he felt. Perhaps it was last weekend at his local bar.

One single, major benefit: You won't ever have to experience that embarrassing moment again.

One inevitable response: Have a clear call to action. Don't tell the reader to call, come into the store, and mail the coupon. That's three freaking instructions, goddamn! Tell the reader to click the button below. Give one clear instruction.

Here's an analogy to demonstrate the power of the Rule of One:
Imagine you're back in the gold rush days. Let's say there was a ton of gold about 6ft underground. You've spoken to friends (prospects) around the community and they've told you they think the gold is in a radius of half a mile. Now picture this:
There's a guy that's digging his face off with a shovel and getting full of dirt. He goes to ten different locations and digs 0.5 ft each. There's the other guy that has the exact same objective, but he has an entirely different approach. He listened to his friends (prospects) and what they told him. I think you can guess what his approach was. Instead of going to loads of different locations, he picked one and hammered it from all different angles. He kept digging and digging until he hit a rock. He came at it from an angle and got it out. He used different tools to hack more dirt out. Little do you know, he struck gold while the other guy is still looking for the good stuff on the surface. I'm sorry, but it doesn't work like that.
So how does this relate to copy? Well, instead of trying to push loads of different emotional buttons with little pressure, you take a sledgehammer and obliterate one dominant emotion. We are getting closer and closer to the good stuff.
Here's a checklist to use for the headline and lead: I got this from Clayton Makepeace. I'm about to show you examples of these in action, so pay attention and read the copy in the pictures carefully.

1. Grab them by the eyeballs

- Flag ideal prospect (same phraseology)
- Spark curiosity (tease, and then some more)
- Present big / most compelling benefit

2. Support and expand headline

- Reinforce the benefit promised
- Continue to stoke curiosity

3. Establish credibility

- Prove that you're a credible ("guru" section) = increased believability (very important in today's market of skepticism)

4. Big promise / bribe

- Promise what will be revealed later

Read the copy of this picture. I'm about to use it as an example.

"WE SNUCK THROUGH!"

18 Little—Known Tax Loopholes and Income Tricks that Made it Through Tax Reform Intact!

Thank God for the reform! President Trump's long-awaited overhaul provided big tax cu for the average American...

But perhaps the best thing he did was allow 18 amazing tax loopholes and income trick to go forward untouched!

A new FREE BOOK reveals how you could collect up to $6,842 per month thanks to these 100% legal ideas...

(NOTE: Limit one free book per household. First come, first served. Please read the letter below for instructions on how to secure your free copy)

---

1. Grab them by the eyeballs

Flag ideal prospect: The promotion is from Agora Financial. Their readers will definitely be interested in saving some more money on tax (benefit). It targets the readers' self-interest and also taps into a pre-existing belief (someone like Wall Street is hiding secrets from them) "Loopholes", "Little-known facts" and "Tricks".

Spark curiosity: The specificity of "18" makes the reader believe and think. "What's this?

How come I don't know about these tax loopholes? And if there's 18, I probably only need 1 to work". It also has a story element, "Made it through". This really gets the curiosity burning in flames.

Present big / most compelling benefit: Save more money by spending less on tax.

2. Support and expand headline

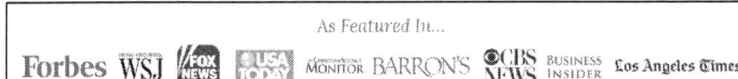

As Featured In...

Forbes WSJ FOX NEWS USA TODAY MONITOR BARRON'S CBS NEWS BUSINESS INSIDER Los Angeles Times

Too the ink has just dried on the President's new tax bill. And, already, Americans are set to see big savings...

The top tax rate dropped 7%...

Everyone gets *twice* the standard deduction...

And Obamacare's individual mandate is finally getting repealed!

But perhaps the biggest benefit of all is *what's NOT getting touched...*

You see, Ted Benna, the 401(k) pioneer responsible for $15 trillion in retirement savings, recently put out a new eye-opening book...

It's called **The "501(k)" Plan: How to Fully Fund Your Own Worry-Free Retirement—Starting at Any Age.**

And, in it, Benna reveals the best places to grow your money to get outsized returns...

These are the little-known secrets politicians, celebrities, and the top fund managers in the world use to dramatically—*and safely*—grow their money...

Often totally outside the stock market!

And, best of all, these strategies all survived the new 1,097-page tax bill intact.

First sentence: "Thank God for the **reform**".

Second sentence: "Was allowed **18 amazing tax loopholes** and income tricks".

Please see second picture: "The ink has just dried on the president's new tax bill and Americans are set to see big savings"

Reinforce the benefit promised: The reader is about to get a free book that will tell him exactly how to use these tax-saving ideas. "FREE BOOK reveals..."

Continue to stoke curiosity: "18 little-known tax loopholes". The writer does it all throughout by keeping the claims "blind". *"The biggest benefit of all is what's NOT getting touched..."*

"These are the little-known secrets politicians, celebrities, and the top fund managers in the world use to dramatically—*and safely*—grow their money..."

3. Establish credibility

Look at the box below. The writer established massive credibility for good ol' Ted Benna. Also look at all the magazines he has been featured on (previous picture).

Who is Ted Benna?

Ted Benna is considered by many as America's #1 expert on retirement savings.

- 1965: Starts career as retirement benefits consultant for high-net worth clients

- 1970s: Offers solution to save pension plans while serving on U.S. Chamber of Commerce's *Employee Benefit Committee*. In 2006, Federal government finally incorporates Benna's idea, 30 years too late...

4. Big promise / bribe

There it is, highlighted. The writer makes a bold promise and then tells you the only way you're going to find this information, is by reading the rest of this letter.

> *You're just a hamster on a wheel—stuck pretty much going nowhere!*
>
> In his new book—which you can get today FOR FREE—Benna shows you where the real money is being made...

THE SALES ARGUMENT

H ere are the basic principles for the body copy: Just remember principles never change, but tactics do.

When it comes to body copy, in most cases, you'll find a way to repeat the same big promise in many ways by breaking it down into specific claims, proving those claims, providing credibility, and answering objections.

PROMISES

The promise is the most fundamental piece in the copy. You can't sell on just logic. The promise is the oxygen of the sales message. Pump those heart cells full of oxygen and you're gonna be ripping at those emotional heart strings. But hey! Don't get carried away. The promise must be believable and—in today's day and age of skepticism growing due to exaggerated claims—a smaller promise that's more believable will outperform a giant promise, especially when it comes to ad networks and compliance.

Once you've tugged those heart fibers, then you can start appealing to the rational mind. That's when you give the prospect the excuses and justifications to buy your product.

The more facts you tell, the more you sell. People buy emotionally and justify the purchase logically. The more facts you can tell, the more reasons and excuses they have for (justifying) the purchase.

Decent copywriters provide benefits. Great copywriters show the reader they have a problem. Readers can get benefits everywhere. There's this little thing called "Google Search". You can find just about anything in the world!

Take the example of "The End of America" promo. They didn't pile promise upon promise, upon promise. In fact, there was very little of it. Rather, they showed the readers they have a serious problem coming and provided tons of proof. One of the main reasons this letter was so effective, is because of the multi- dimensional approach. Here's what I mean:

Most people will say the writer, Mike Palmer, really hammered the emotion of fear. And that's certainly the case. But as you'll find out later, these emotions go in tandem with each other. Like Yin and Yang. He also gave the reader confidence that he can take advantage of this opportunity and actually make some money in the process. Now he has appealed to fear and greed simultaneously. What a deadly combo that is!

Here's the main reason why this works:

Think about the two primary factors that cause humans to act and what motivates them. Number one is to move away from pain and two is to move towards gain. Pain is more motivating and you want to solve it with serious urgency. However, when it comes to pleasure, there's no real urgency to it. For example, when people want to achieve a sense of pleasure like losing weight, most of the time they don't take action. But… if you can make the prospect feel the pain of something, they will be in a great mental state to take action.

You can't just write about the benefits. C'mon, that's level 1. Show the reader he has a serious problem and then agitate it— take some salt and aggressively smudge it into the wound. But remember, you must first create the wound. Damn, that got a little dark for a second (you get the point, though). Let's push on.

The 4 Different Promises

- Big Promise: 21 Days to six pack abs.
- Small Promise: How to keep your money from being murdered.
- Direct Promise: How to earn $10,000 a week.
- Indirect / Implied Promise: There's a new railroad across America, and it's making some people very rich…

A great sales letter will include all / most of these promises (coming from the big main promise). Also, just a side note: The indirect and implied promise seems to be getting some traction, especially on more skeptical audiences that have had enough of huge hyped-up promises. Look at this easy example:

- Lose weight quickly (big promise).
- Lose weight on your legs (small promise).
- Lose weight in 7 days and get beach ready (direct promise).

CLAIMS

Claims are statements that support your promises. Never make your claims bigger than your proof. Always have at least two proof elements after each claim. Preferably three to five if you can. And please, avoid cringey phrases like "get rich quick", "lose weight instantly"—just lower the tone.

It all goes back to the prospect awareness. If he has heard the same claim repeatedly, he will automatically tune out as soon as he hears something similar. That said, you can embed the "If…then" statement to make your claim more believable. It provides logical proof and bypasses the "yeah, sure" detector. It makes it feel like this would only work for the reader. I'll cover the "If…then" statement in much more detail later. Here's an example:

"**If** you have 10 hours a month to spare, **this** side gig could be the perfect opportunity to grow a six-figure income".

Bear in mind, the "If… then" statement includes all of the target readers. The writer knows the target prospect has more than ten hours a month and is looking to start a passive income stream. Never include an "If, then" statement if you don't know your target reader intimately. You need to hit the nail on the head when you apply this tactic. If you don't know the target market well enough, the promotion will bomb right outta the gate. Here's another example: "*If you have a knack for keeping track of things, **the** world needs you!*"

See, the writer knows the reader has a knack of keeping track of things, otherwise he wouldn't have used it.

Just to reiterate, because it's so important: Instead of making bigger promises that will generate hype and skepticism, pile layer upon layer of proof to support each claim. Without belief, the prospect won't buy. In simple terms, your claims are the glue that support your promises, and the proof acts as the framework to keep the picture intact.

WORDS TO CONTROL YOUR PROSPECTS MIND

These "mind control" words kill two birds with one stone. First, they act as "legal" words. Second, they're killer for persuasion. It's all good to make great big claims, but what's the use if it doesn't pass legal requirements? The copy will never be published in the first place. And that's why I'm about to tell you how to make a claim sound mouth-watering while still passing legal.

DISCLAIMER: I am not a lawyer or anything of the sort. Please take further advice from your lawyer about legal requirements. This is just an observation. Okay, now that I've got the obvious disclaimer out the way, here's what I've discovered after dissecting hundreds of sales letters, particularly from the financial niche. Think about how you can apply this in your niche.

To make promises and claims that will get the readers' emotions rushing - without breaking any laws - you need to embed what I call "disclaimer" words. For example, you'll see Agora use words like: "Could have", "how you could start today with as little as $50", "Virtually unheard of", "potentially", "almost", "Up to"..., "As far as I know…"

Look at the picture: Here the writers uses two disclaimer words "some" and "as much as". This may not seem like a big deal, but here's what's actually happening.

> **It's never too late to get started.**
> **Some people nearing retirement age are receiving**
> **payments for as much as $29,000, $37,000,**
> **even as high as $57,000!**

When the reader reads this sub headline, he makes his own conclusion that he can earn that amount of money. In effect, the writer hasn't actually said that the reader WILL earn this amount of money; he is subtly implying that it COULD happen, but the reader fills in the gap. The fact that he also said "some people" also tells you that not everyone has done this. At this point though, the reader will definitely not be thinking logically.

PROOF

When it comes to proof, most beginner copywriters think that testimonials and social proof are the only forms of proof.

In fact, when I first started out, I thought exactly the same. Whenever people said you had to insert a lot of proof, I just thought that meant tons of testimonials. Luckily, there's way more than two proof elements. Proof and credibility merges together. If you provide proof, it will also increase credibility.

Proof is a very important piece of your copy, especially as everyone is becoming increasingly skeptical from all the ads. The greater the promise, the more proof is required. Just take "The End of America" promo as an example. I believe it was like a fifty- page sales letter or something along those lines. It's a big promise they were making. Hence, they spent fifty pages providing proof upon proof, until they had a bulletproof argument. Here are all the proof elements:

1. Dramatic demonstration

This is the (GREATEST FORM OF PROOF). And don't take my word for it, the famous "Claude Hopkins" said it as well. Here's the reason why it works: You know Tony Robbins, right? Well, one of the main reasons why he blew up in popularity is largely due to his demonstrations on live TV.

Think about it: If someone was suffering from a phobia their whole entire life and in the TV studio, Tony Robbins helps them overcome it almost immediately… What does this do? Well, knowing that people believe what they SEE, Tony almost becomes like this God-like person. This little demonstration shows the typical before and after state. It couldn't be more powerful.

But in written form, you can't physically demonstrate the product? You're in luck! We can work around this. There's a way that you can get your prospect to demonstrate your products for themselves without ever letting them touch it! How? I'll tell you when we talk more about storytelling. On that note, let's talk more about...

2. Before and after stories

This can come in many forms:

- **Personality (story of the guru):** You'll see this one a lot. It typically goes like this in the business opportunity niche. "I was broke, discovered this solution, now I'm rich". Oh, and by the way, the product is always the "GUIDE" that helped them get the result.

- **3rd party testimonial**: Shows how someone achieved their desired result with the product that is being sold.

3. Living proof

If you're in the business opportunity niche and you're showing people how they can travel the world and work where they want, you better be demonstrating how you're living their desired lifestyle (end results). Instead of filming videos in your bedroom, it would be a wise decision to shoot these videos at exotic locations all over the world.

4. Social proof

There are a couple of ways that you can apply this. **Images:** Agora does this all the time. They'll show a picture of the GURU on TV.

This builds credibility and provides a lot of social proof. It implies that he is someone of significance and has helped many other people.

Words: Look at the difference between these two paragraphs and pay attention to the images they conjure in your mind. This text is for a call to action:

*"Here's what to do next: Call 07232032032 and **give** the telephone operators the CODE. **They're standing by and waiting for your call**".*

*"Here's what to do next: Call 07232032032. **If** the telephone operators can't get to your call right away, **please wait a moment as the lines may be very busy**".*

The first paragraph gives the image of the telephone operators just sitting at their desk talking shit and playing with their thumbs eagerly waiting for a call. The second one gives the image of very busy telesales workers and they're constantly on the phone.

The second one provides much more social proof, right? The word **"If"** is responsible for most of this. It implies that there's high demand and other people are taking action and calling in. If you can think of ways to show other people have already taken a similar action you want the reader to take, you'll be good to go with social proof.

5. Reasons why

All throughout this book, I've used this proof element. How many times have you seen me say "Here's why..."? A lot, right! Reason why" copy works like gangbusters and it's a natural form of communication. Whenever someone provides a reason why, it gives more justification to the statement.

Here's a simple way to do it:

Follow your **"because"** with compelling reasons. This is the most ethical form of persuasion because people always act in their own self-interest. See what I did there? Ahhh, it works! Give...

1. Reasons why your product is superior to others.
2. Reasons to believe that what you say is true.
3. Reasons to take action today. This is a big one!

Whenever you inject some urgency or scarcity, you need to provide a **REASON WHY**! You can't just say there's "250 copies left". They've heard it all before, trust me. Rather say...

"There's 250 copies left, because I've just made an arrangement with my book publisher to roll out a test campaign. Their printer can only print 250 copies and they can only ship 250 copies for test campaigns". Doesn't that sound a whole lot more believable?

Tell him WHY: Why you are writing to him, why FREE, and why it costs what it does. "Reason why" copy is also a natural way to overcome objections and answer the questions in the reader's mind, naturally at that point. It helps you stay one step ahead of your reader. Just imagine he is skeptical to everything you're saying. Pretend he is giving you a "yeah sure" after every claim. Look at this example: The reader will be thinking, "Why are you giving away so much value for free?" The use of the **REASON WHY** *"we need your repeat business"* covers the objection.

As well as all of the gifts I've discussed today — including your copy of my *Marijuana Millionaire Playbook*!

You may be wondering...

Why am I giving away so much value for such a great price?

Well, here's the bare-naked, warts-and-all truth...

At $49 we risk losing money. To turn a profit, we need your repeat business.

---

6. Charts and graphs (must be simple and easy)

Listen, your reader doesn't want to spend his time making sense of a complex chart or graph. Just make it really easy to understand. Simplicity is key when it comes to persuasion.

That's why a lot of the copywriting books talk about writing at third-grade level. They refer to the Flesch Kinkaid score and it needs to be approximately 5.0 and lower. Apply the same concept here. The fact that it's so simple also provides more of a logical argument.

Let's talk about **reframing**. A lot of times you'll see graphs that will refer to a timeline of "weeks" and then provide another one that refers to "years". This builds more desire because it shows the reader the massive potential gain. Carefully read the text below the graph. The writer **REFRAMED** the potential gains.

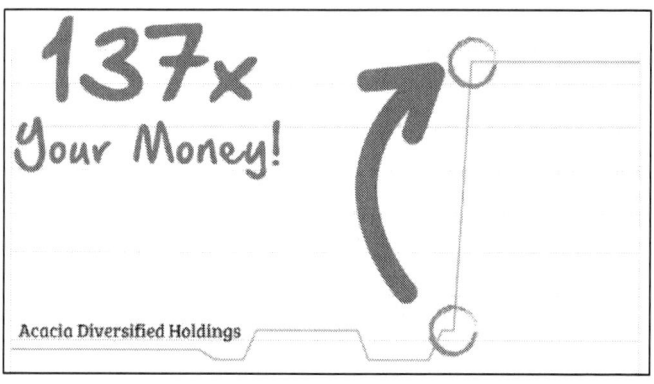

Had you put $100 in when shares were trading for just pocket change...

You could have turned your $100 stake into a quick $13,700 windfall.

Invest $1,000 and you'd be looking at **$137,000 in profits!**

Imagine that... six figures in gains in just a few short weeks.

Can you see that? He reframed the profit gain by changing the amount that's invested. From **$100** (second sentence) to **$1000** (third sentence). The reader will be more focused on the huge number of potential profits, and most likely glance over the larger number required for the investment.

7. Explain the mechanism (explain the underlying theory and why it works)

Back to the mechanism. Here you really want to build intrigue and make the mechanism the holy grail, so to say. It's the reason why the prospect will get their desired end results. It acts as the vehicle that will take them to their destination.

Although you want the mechanism to sound as simple as possible and anybody can do it, on the other side of the coin, you also want to do the opposite. You want to show the prospect that it's not going to be very easy if he does it by himself. You need to communicate that he needs your help, and it can be done in a few ways:

Show complexity – Use complicated jargon and complex-looking images that the reader can't make sense of on his own. Take this example:

- Trend and moving averages…
- Volatility swing measurements…
- Momentum shifts…
- Volume action…
- Relative strength and stochastic metrics, and…
- Regression analysis.

But be very careful. After pulling the prospect along gently by showing him how easy it is, don't push him over the cliff by now making everything else in the sales letter complex. It's like salt. You just want to drop a little pinch in the mix, not a handful.

8. Scientific study

This really doesn't need much explanation. All you need to do is find a study that proves your claim and refer to it. "Take a look at this study..."

9. Quote expert or authority

Make sure the reader knows about this authoritative person. If they're well known like Warren Buffett, that's great! There's nothing worse than finding a quote from some unknown person. It still provides some proof, I guess. Anyways, make sure the quote is concise and specific. There's no point in finding a quote that doesn't actually prove your claim.

> "If You Don't Find a Way to Make Money While You Sleep, You Will Work Until You Die."
> *— Warren Buffett*

10. Testimonials

You might get a little squeamish over this, so hold tight. Whenever you're getting a testimonial, make sure that you're in control. You don't want a testimonial that says, "Dane was great!" That's almost as good as no testimonial at all. You really want to take charge and direct the person giving the testimonial. You can get on the phone and ask specific questions that will overcome objections and identify with the reader. Every piece of your copy must further the sale.

For example, if the target prospect has an objection over time or money, you ask the client providing the testimonial, "How has this product helped you overcome your previous problem with a lack of money?"

Client: *"Before I bought your copywriting system, I always struggled to make money. It was always through hard physical labor and working for an asshole of a boss. I didn't have the financial skill that brings in more money. But once I finished your copywriting system, I got one client and it already paid for itself".*

This a lot better than "Dane was great!" It **identifies** with the target reader and overcomes the objection of investing in the course as well. How about that? Now we're talking!

Another option is to change the testimonial yourself with the client's permission. There's nothing unethical about this. If the prospect has communicated that he was in a poor financial situation and the product was actually the vehicle that dragged him out of that slum, there's no harm in forming a testimonial that communicates that point but in a more persuasive way. All you have to do is ask the past customer for permission. You will still be communicating the same thing. "Could I have your permission to do this?" Most of the time, they'll say "YES!"

Each testimonial should show one major benefit, identify with the reader, and overcome objections.

- **Customer results testimonials:** "I worked with Dane and in the first 2 weeks he increased my response by 87%".

- **Customer experience testimonials:** "Before I met Dane, we struggled to get more customers and couldn't find someone to help with customer acquisition. It was a real joy".

- **Expert testimonials**—Jay Abraham: "Dane is a great copywriter".

- **Case studies:** One of my clients increased their front-end promotion by 10% after they'd made a simple change recommended by me.

11. Logical argument

Example: *"It just doesn't make sense to invest in anything else but "pot stocks"*. An easy way to appeal to logic is to use words like: "The reason for".., "Simply because", "This has been proved by thousands", "It's simple…", "Here's why", "And", "Because", "In fact", "Think about it", "Of course". Later, you'll learn much more about logic and the underlying structures. Remember you must start with something they agree with. You can't make a logical argument like this at the start of the sales letter. First, you haven't built any desire or anticipation and secondly, they won't believe this right out the gate. Once you've made statements the reader can agree with, they will be more susceptible to accept new ones.

12. Product / company history (the process of making the prod uct - *Blood Sweat and Tears*)

Just look at this example: The writer is describing the entire process they had to go through to create this product. They even had to make a $2.4 million deal and "it didn't come cheap". Telling the story and process of creating the product increases the perceived value of the product. Now that the reader knows they spent so much money, it becomes a steal when they can get it for $49.

And that's Why We Made a $2.4 Million Deal

You see...

The members of the Six-Sigma test were able to make so much money...

We were eager to share the power of the system with other lucky Americans...

But it didn't come cheap....

Because the prestigious financial firm that made this possible has worked with some of the top hedge funds on the planet.

You might know the mysterious hedge fund Renaissance Technologies.

Founded by a cold war code breaker, Renaissance is NOT your typical hedge fund.

Take the Mona Lisa painting as an example. The painting itself is just a picture. To someone that has never heard of the Mona Lisa and is completely unaware of it, they might think it will sell for around twenty bucks. It's the story of this painting that makes it so valuable.

13. News items

Just relate the claim to recent news events. For example, "The price of bricks is about to rise because Trump has just mentioned he is about to build another 500 million houses".

14. Acknowledge disbelief

"I was skeptical, too… until I saw this + (proof element).
"I was skeptical, too, until I saw my son making $1,239 per week with Amazon drop shipping".

15. Specificity

If you don't get anything else from these proof elements, remember this one; it's vital if you want to persuade. Whenever you can, be specific. Don't say "this company made $1000 this week". Go and do your research, find the company name, location, and the exact amount of revenue they made.

"Shark Inc, in Baltimore, Maryland just made $1375.56 this week" —it sounds believable! Specifics bring up images in the readers' minds. If you said "gun", it's a very different image than "Gold AK-47", isn't it? You can see the second one in your mind's eye.

Specificity is the KEY to BELIEVABILITY. And if the prospect doesn't believe you, he won't buy. Whenever you've written your first and second draft, go over the entire piece and see if you can make anything more specific. Oh, by the way, don't be silly about this. Don't take it too far and provide numbers with seven decimal points "34.744393". "34.74" will do!

Inclusion statements (if and then) also act as a form of specificity when you can provide a very specific solution to a very specific problem. *"**If** you're a fifty-year-old male and suffering from arthritis in both knees, **then** this product is exactly for you"*.

16. Statistics and data

Make it simple and easy to understand. That's it!

17. Analogy

Metaphors and stories are powerful selling tools. Metaphors act as a form of proof and is one of the best tools to change your prospects' beliefs. Remember, you do not want the reader to react with resistance. You do this by giving them a good time and so you enter into agreement without them ever feeling "sold". The "pushy salesmen" detector is not activated, because you're not talking about them! All the magic happens in the unconscious mind. It automatically gets emotionally involved. The mind concentrates on the ideas / concepts in the metaphor and spots symbolism. If a metaphor is symbolic of a previous experience in a person's life, the person will relate the story to their situation. You don't even have to consciously point it out! Their unconscious mind does that for you!

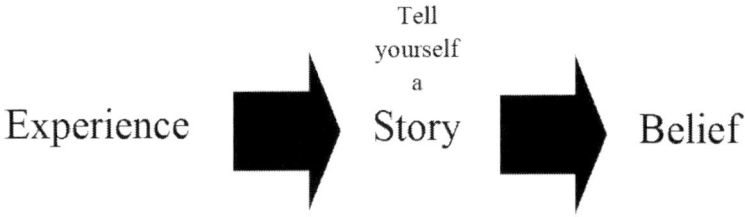

Look at this example from the famous hypnotist, Milton Erickson. He told this story to an alcoholic patient who subsequently stopped drinking:

Milton E: Usually, I send alcoholic patients to AA because AA can do a better job than I can do. An alcoholic came to me and he said...

Patient: My grandparents on both sides were alcoholics; my parents were alcoholics; my wife's parents were alcoholics; my wife is an alcoholic, and I have had delirium tremors eleven times. I am sick of being an alcoholic. My brother is an alcoholic too. Now that is a hell of a job for you. What do you think you can do about it?

Milton E: I asked him what his occupation was.

Patient: When I am sober, I work on a newspaper. And alcohol is an occupational hazard there.

Milton E: All right, you want me to do something about it - with that history. Now, the thing I am going to suggest to you won't seem the right thing. You go out to the Botanical Gardens. You look at all the cactus there and marvel at cactus that can survive three years without water, without rain. And do a lot of thinking.

Milton E: Many years later, a young woman came in and said,

"Dr. Erickson, you knew me when I was three years old. I moved to California when I was three years old. Now I am in Phoenix and I came to see what kind of a man you were - what you looked like".

I said, "Take a good look, and I'm curious to know why you want to look at me".

She said, "Any man who would send an alcoholic out to the Botanical Gardens to look around, to learn how to get around without alcohol, and have it work, is the kind of man I want to see! My mother and father have been sober ever since you sent my father out there".

"What is your father doing now?"

"He's working for a magazine. He got out of the newspaper business. He says the newspaper business has an occupational hazard of alcoholism".

I want to point out a few things here: The **experiences** and elements of the story relate directly to the patient. In the **story,** the father suffered the exact same experience the patient was going through and was now at the end result the patient desired. It inspired **belief**. This suggestion is indirect through the symbolic story. The symbol being the cactus, and how it can go without "drinking" (water) for such a long time. The cactus has nothing to do with drinking and alcoholism itself, so prompts zero resistance.

The Formula for Life Changing Metaphors:

1. Identify what *EXPERIENCE* the prospect needs for a change of perspective.

2. Give him the *EXPERIENCE* through imagined experience in his mental movie OR an external real-world experience.

Knowing the prospect is the key to telling the right selling story. When you're using metaphors and analogies, make sure they're widely known, and the reader is familiar with them. Familiar facts help build belief and it's the golden key to persuasion. It's a pretty good idea to cast a wide net. Most people have experienced the feeling of swimming in the sea. Few people have had the experience of dieting to 5% body fat.

18. Creative guarantees

"If you don't see X result in X time frame and you've done everything we've told you, send us an email and we will refund all the money and you keep the product". It's not an obvious proof element, but it shows that you have skin in the game.
Take this example:
"If you don't see your income increase 5 times in the next 6 months, you keep the product and all the bonuses ($100 tablet + 1-year FREE membership). You don't even have to ship anything back. Just send me a quick email with the subject line "REFUND".
This acts a strong proof element. It implies that what you're selling will definitely work, otherwise you wouldn't be doing this!

19. Address flaws (increases believability for other claims and builds trust)

This is very powerful, but you need to apply it strategically. Address the flaw and then pivot to an advantage (benefit). For example, you might say: *"The price of the copywriting course is not cheap. **That's why** I've decided to give you an option for three monthly payments and 100% lifetime money back guarantee".*

Did you see what happened there? I addressed the concern and then pivoted by using the words "That's why…"

20. Use permissive language in your headline or promise

Compare the difference:

"This **WILL** get you fifty more customers per week".

Versus…

"This **MAY** get you fifty more customers per week".

The word "MAY" is a lot softer and adds more believability. This "softer language" is powerful in today's age of increasing skepticism.

That's at least nineteen pieces of proof! Wow! That's much better than just testimonials and social proof. Before we move onto the hidden powers of credibility, I want to emphasize a few points:

You're really trying to insert a variety of proofs - some facts, studies, quotes from credible sources, testimonials, analogies. Using all kinds of proof will give your argument much more authority and believability. Not sure if you've heard this saying, but it's called "death by a thousand cuts". That's exactly what you must do when it comes to proof elements. You keep chipping away subtly until the resistance collapses.

BUILDING TRUST AND CREDIBILITY

T here are tons of ways to create more credibility. Here are just a few:

Self-granted credentials: "England's Most Expensive Copy-writer".

Qualifications: "PhD in Copywriting".

Product Specialization: Special products for every problem.

Customized Labels: Protein for Women, Protein for Men Over 40. (same ingredients different label).

Put yourself in environments that begs authority: Standing up on stage, TV, Featured in popular websites / magazines.

Borrow credibility: Give away an authority figure's product as a bonus. For example, if you were selling tennis products give away Roger Federer's wrist band.

Photographs: When selecting pictures for a marketing campaign, make sure you're selling the reader the result they desire. Every piece of your copy must sell!

BURN THIS INTO YOUR BRAIN:
You're not selling xyz 'benefit'. You're selling the AFTER. You're selling – what life COULD BE. Paint the picture in his mind and SHOW him (don't just tell). Don't be abstract. You're selling the emotions he feels when stepping out of the car (picture to the right).

To build trust, it's a good idea to have a headshot photo, so the prospect knows he's getting this information from a "real" person.

Technicality (show complexity): It implies the ONLY way to get the desired result is with the product and the help of the guru.

Product track Record (customer satisfaction, safety record): Show the customer's previous results and how satisfied they were. Tell them how long you've been in business and show any five-star inspections / reviews. Give 'em the history of the successful product.

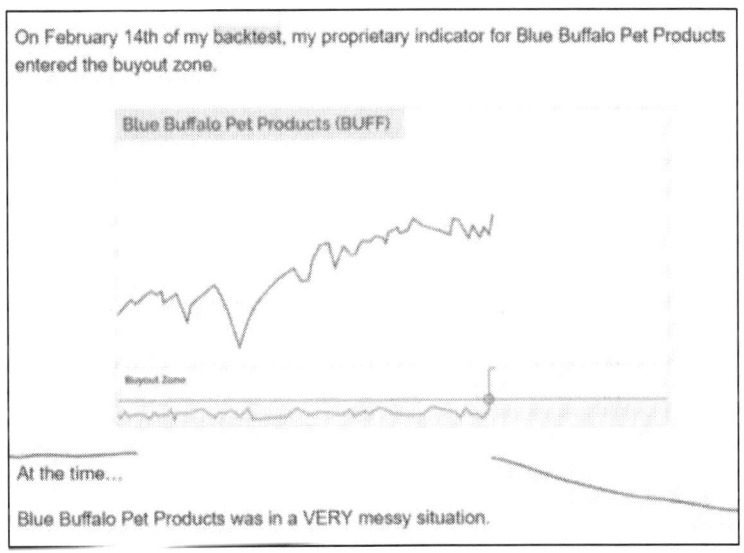

Agora Financial also uses "back tests" to show the product track record. This is very powerful because it allows the writer to show the large potential gains the reader **could** experience... while at the same time, still passing the legal requirements. The writer isn't saying the prospect WILL experience these gains; he is merely highlighting what the back tests have shown. Of course, the prospect fills the rest of the picture with his own conclusion, "Wow! I can earn as much as $10,000! This "indicator" is great".

GURU TRACK RECORD (PREDICTIONS)

Make no mistake; of course, the writer is just hand picking all the right predictions. There's no possible way someone can always be accurate on their predictions. So, although, the "guru" predicted the boom of Facebook, he probably made tons of other wrong predictions. This isn't necessarily unethical, because the writer isn't lying. He isn't saying the guru hasn't made an incorrect prediction. He just chooses not to mention it. The reader makes his own conclusion, "He has predicted all of these! Man, this guy must be right on all of them". They forget to think critically about all the other wrong predictions.

I've made some pretty bold predictions that have come true.

Over the last 20 years I've been spot on about the events that have reshaped our economy...

I predicted Facebook would become a $100 billion company.

I went back on CNBC and predicted we were headed to 20,000.

What do you know? The highest closing record for the Dow was 26,828.39, set on October 3, 2018.

I was right about crypto too!

OVERCOMING OBJECTIONS

T here are many ways to overcome objections in copy, and we're going to cover them in just a second.

First, I want to mention the main difference between a word class copywriter and a dirt-poor copywriter that blows his claims as big as balloons and eventually pops the prospects' believability bubble.
Here it is:
A great copywriter knows that objections are best handled before they're even conscious! They understand all the objections, and **where** they're most likely to come up in the selling process. They cover them in logical order. You see, any average person can list a load of objections and randomly overcome them in the copy. The great copywriters do it as the objection arises at that point in time.
Take this example:
"How to Make $10,000 with one Sales Funnel"—If this was seen by an average person off the street that has never been exposed to "funnels", they won't have a clue what it is... and it needs to be addressed first before handling any other objections. This is important, especially if it's a complex or unusual topic. Just think about it: how many (front-end) sales letters have you seen that addresses the price upfront? None!
Here's an example of overcoming objections in logical order. After making a big promise, the first objection the reader is going to have on his mind is, "How much will it cost me?" and "Do I need to have special connections?" This won't be the case for everyone, but Agora Financial readers would definitely bring these up. Again, it goes back to knowing your target customer.

Dear Reader,

What's better than making money?

Making money on your own terms…

Working when you want…

Where you want…

Without a boss, a fixed schedule or a glass ceiling.

But how do you do this?

And how do you do it without having special connections…

And with little financial risk?

After a few more lines, the writer covers some more objections:

If you're creative, you can get started with $0 and launch risk-free. You get orders and buyers before you spend a cent... and you can get started today using just a few hours a week.

All the objections are covered in logical order. The writer didn't start of by answering the objection "What's the catch?" It wouldn't make sense. The prospect doesn't even know the details of the offer and what the product can do for him. It would feel terribly incongruent and out of place. Also, by covering these objections in their logical order, it keeps the reader's attention because he isn't distracted with a nagging uncovered objection in his mind.

Put another way: Throughout the sales message, you'll need to know **where** the prospect is most likely to have questions, see roadblocks, or raise objections that might prevent them from moving forward. Right when the objection is coming up, you find a way to put something in place that will handle it before it becomes conscious.

Now, here's a little hint that should help:

As you go through your copy—either the outline you put together before you write, or the draft copy after it's written— get into the mind of your prospect. And, from their perspective, question every claim, proof, and promise. After every claim, you can say "So what?!" or "Bull!", "Yeah, sure!" This will show you whether you need to add more proof. By the way, as I mentioned earlier, 'reason why' copy is great for overcoming objections and concerns. For example:

"There are only 100 copies left".
*"There are only 100 copies left **because** my book publisher can only send 100 copies per shipment".*

If this all sounds too complicated, don't worry; there's an easier and more formulaic way. I got this from Agora Financial (Joe Schrieffer). It's called Copy Boarding (very similar to story boarding).

Step #1 - Your Pitch

Hook the prospect and reel him in. Imagine this: A father goes fishing to catch some bass with his son. He's not the most experienced, but he knows that he needs to choose certain bait that will attract this kind of fish. That's all handled.

They both rushed to the mossy bank and spent the entire afternoon, but caught no fish. While sitting in their half-broken camping chairs, they had a few "close calls" where they almost caught a fish. The son even saw the small "bite" on the rod. This father drives back home in his red Chevy and calls his friend who is an expert fisherman, and tells him the story. The expert fisherman spoke in an almost sarcastic tone and said... "You need to hook the fish first". Once you've sunk the hook into its mouth, then it can't escape. It's captivated and engaged. This is exactly what you need to be doing to your prospects. Just like you'll need different hooks for different sized fish, you'll need different hooks for different markets. Test out different hooks and see which one your prospects respond to best.

Step #2 - The Objections

Once you've got a killer hook, get a 5x5 index card or post-it note. Think of every single objection that might occur and write each one down. Even better, if you've got tons of objections from current, past, and future customers, use that.

Don't be afraid here, just write. If you're struggling for ideas, you can even go on forums and Facebook groups to look for potential objections. Or kindly ask your prospects, "Why haven't you signed up for [insert product]"—they'll give you some objections.

Step #3—The Organization

At this point, you've sunk the hook so deep into the fish's (prospect's) mouth and stacked all the cards in your favor. You're in the process of reeling this bad boy in, but there's a few more things to do. Now, we need to get our shit together and get organized. This is where we put all the objections in logical order. Like this:

The first few objections are often related to time (fifth sentence) and money (second and third sentence).

Minting hundreds of new millionaires — and even billionaires, like Christian Blue and Michael Kennedy — along the way.

And because many of these marijuana stocks are still trading for just pennies...

You could literally start investing in marijuana stocks with just a $100 bill...

Turn that tiny stake into a massive fortune...

And retire incredibly wealthy in less than a year.

Followed by, "Can I trust you?" – That's where the credibility comes in.

> Look, I'm one of the most well-connected folks in the marijuana industry today...
>
> I'm constantly brought on by the world's largest news sources, like Fox Business, to explain the things they can't about marijuana...

After covering more objections in the body copy, the next few might be internal hang ups, like "I'm not a professional investor, so I can't do this". And then lastly, the offer section, where the writer will address the price, risk and "What's the catch?" objections. So, you organize the objections in a logical format so that you take the biggest objections at the top, and the more specific ones are at the bottom of the sales process.

Step #4 - Write Benefit Driven Sub Headlines

Now we plug and play! Well, not quite so easy. Here's where you need to write:

1. Benefit-driven subheads.
2. Overcome objections.

Take this example:

> This is why "Weed-tirement" is so exciting.
> This strategy allows you to build a marijuana fortune without having to gamble on high-risk stocks.

Benefit: Become a millionaire with marijuana stocks.

Objection: "Will I lose a lot of money, if I invest in marijuana stocks?"

The words following "without" are responsible for overcoming the objection. Pretty straightforward, isn't it?

Step #5 - The "Fill In"

Fill in all the missing parts and pieces of your sales letter once you have your objections laid out and organized correctly. In a nutshell:

Brainstorm all the objections your prospects will have in regards to your product ahead of time. Organize them based on the order in which they will come up. From there, your sales page is just a matter of resolving one objection after the next.

You'll see copywriters do this all the time (front-end promo's):

They'll build credibility for the guru or personality before introducing price. Because "why should I listen to you?" is the objection that pops up before "how much does this cost?".

Laying them out in the order they pop up in your reader's head is vital. Because while A, B, and C are phenomenal benefits, not all of them matter to your reader. Not yet. Right now, you've got to direct your attention to objection A. Because that's the nagging doubt in your prospect's mind. Until that's overcome, you won't have a single chance of making a sale.

I know I'm literally repeating the same point over again, but it needs to sink in. Again, it comes down to structure and the chain links of belief. Once you've resolved the first objection, you can then lead him logically through the rest. Some more pro tips to find objections:

- Ask the prospects that didn't buy, why that was the case.
- Ask the customer who did buy—what their initial concerns were.
- Live Q and A to test objections before writing the sales message.

I've seen a few people do this really well. They'll go live on a social media platform and in a playful way, ask their audience why they wouldn't buy a certain product. They would comment something like "I have a family to look after, and haven't got time", "I live too far away", or "I can't afford it".

Of course, you don't begin the live call outright like this...First, you'll provide value and then only after, can you do this playful extraction of objections. It's even easier if you're in the business niche, because then you can use your audience as an example and ask for all their objections, and then teach them how to overcome them. That way, they learn, and you get their objections. It's a WIN-WIN!

9 WAYS TO OVERCOME OBJECTIONS

1. Before the sales message

Objection: "Can I trust you?"

You might be thinking "hang on a second, this isn't how to overcome objections in copy". You're right! However, like I've said before, you need to make two sales. First, you need to create a bond between the reader and yourself or the guru. This can be done by sharing the same criteria or values. You do this by publishing free value-based content with an intended message. This way, you build more trust before you even have to "pitch" the prospect.

It also makes the sale a whole lot easier, by the way. By following this process of publishing, you establish an omnipresence in your target market. I won't go too much in depth here, but when you publish content, just make sure you make content that will attract the right target customer.

For example, if you want to work with already established business owners running $1m per month businesses, you're not going to have videos talking about "how to go from $0 to $100k".

2. Headline

If you choose to overcome objections in your headline, make sure they're the dominant ones. It's the first few words the prospect will read. For example: The two biggest objections: "Don't have enough time to write copy" and "Can't afford to hire an expensive copywriter". Headline to overcome these two objections:
"How to Write All Your Video Sales Letters, Emails, and Upsells in as little as 20 minutes without hiring an expensive copywriter".

Let's travel back in time to the start-up days of Domino's Pizza. They knew that customers who were ordering pizza were getting frustrated because they couldn't get their pizza fast enough. What did Domino's do? They gave the customer exactly what they asked for and featured it smack bang in the headline.

"Fresh hot pizza to your door in 30 minutes or less or it's free".

As you can see, they overcame the most common objection- "delivery time". The rest, as they say, is history.

Keep in mind when you're writing indirect leads for front-end offers, you're not really trying to overcome objections in the headline. At least not directly stated, like the copywriting example above. That would be an offer best suited to prospects that already trust you. Remember, you don't want to telegraph the prospect that he is reading a sales message. If he has never heard of you and sees a headline, *"Here's how to invest in the new railroad stock with less than a $50 bill"*, what will he think?

Compare that with, *"There's a new railroad across America, and it's making some people very rich..."* The second one feels more like a story or article than anything, whereas the first screams a pitch. Always think about the awareness and sophistication of the prospect. The first headline is fine for "warm" and "hot" prospects; definitely not for "cold".

3. Body copy: Direct or Indirect

Here's an example of covering the objections indirectly. The writer doesn't come out and say "how much does it cost to invest in this?"—rather, he uses a more indirect approach "trading for just pennies".

> And because many of these marijuana stocks are still trading for just pennies...
>
> You could literally start investing in marijuana stocks with just a $100 bill...
>
> Turn that tiny stake into a massive fortune...
>
> And retire incredibly wealthy in less than a year.

When you're covering objections, both directly or indirectly, you need to know the actual objections the reader would have. You can't afford to cover objections the reader wouldn't ever have. You've got to hit the bull's eye every time. When dissecting sales letters, you'll see the writer overcomes one major objection in many ways.

For example, he wouldn't say "start investing in marijuana stock with just a $100 bill" twenty times. Instead, he will use different language to communicate the same thing.

Here's what I mean: Look at all three sentences. Can you see the similarities? They all hammer the same phrase: **"single $100 bill"**.

> You could get started with a single $100 bill...

> One that could turn *a single $100 bill* into a **retirement fortune**.

> But had you invested a single $100 bill when shares were trading for just 3 cents...

Take this example, where the writer addresses the objection head on:

> These are just two of the secrets you'll discover inside Ted Benna's latest book, **The "501(k)" Plan: How to Fully Fund Your Own Worry-Free Retirement—Starting at Any Age**, which outlines a brand-new retirement solution called the "501(k)."
>
> What is the "501(k)"?

This tends to be done when you know with certainty that the prospect is going to have this particular objection. It also makes logical sense, because in the previous sentence, he mentioned a brand-new concept that no one knows about.

Logically, the next objection will be, "What's the 501k?"

4. Stories

I was going to give you a short little teaser about the impact of storytelling in copy and leave you in the dirt salivating. But you know what... I feel generous today. Let me fully explain storytelling, why it's so effective, and how you can use it to overcome objections.

You're Invited

Want to learn more about stories that sell? If so, I'd like to invite you to read my book *Story Selling Secrets* at:
https://daneknightonbook.com/story-selling-secrets/

First things first: You don't tell a story for the sake of it. As I keep harping on... every piece of copy must further the sale! You must carefully construct the story to **identify with the prospect**. You can do this by using yourself, the "guru", or a third person testimonial.

Oh by the way - You should never talk down to your prospect and tell him it's his fault for not achieving what he wants. That's where stories are so effective.

So, why is storytelling so powerful?

It replaces the story the reader is telling themselves and inspires faith. You see, all of us are walking around every day telling ourselves a story. Perhaps you're telling yourself that "business is hard and not worth doing". The person just fifty metres away from you could be telling themselves a completely different story; "Isn't life just great! You can run successful businesses and live with total freedom".

Where do you think religious beliefs derive from? Just think of the sheer number of stories in the bible. Countless! From these stories, people start to believe in them and then begin telling themselves the same stories. Whether they're accurate or not, is subjective from person to person. What does this have to do with copywriting and making dough? A lot! What you're about to witness will blow your mind. I haven't seen anyone do anything like this in a book. I'm about to break down a complete testimonial story to show how it overcomes objections and shifts the target prospect's worldview. Keep in mind, this was a promotion from Agora Financial and their target reader is an older folk aged between 55-75. This avatar is looking to retire, wants to travel the world, and spend quality time with their partner and kids before he passes away.

Let's dive in:

"Hi, I'm Lucy Jones and I made this video because I know **a lot of you watching are skeptical**" —

[Yes! The target market is skeptical of being scammed. They've been "burned" so many times in their lifetime.]

"and I get it" —

[Showing empathy—not telling the reader he is wrong (agreement frame)]

"There's so much out there that just doesn't work" —

[Reader feels exactly like this.]

"But I'm <u>living proof</u> that the side hustles in Julian's new book actually do work" —

[Transition "BUT" into the SOLUTION—the PRODUCT]

"They worked for me and they can work for you" —

[Gives HOPE! Reader thinks, "She is exactly like me, if she can do it so can I".]

"You see, not that long ago, **money** was a **stressor** for me". —

[She has achieved the same desired result the reader wants.]

"It wasn't like I was poor by any means, but I didn't have enough to spare and do all the things that I really wanted to do" —

[Yep, the reader can relate.]

"And that's when my son told me about something he was doing"

[Soft transition + "son" makes it not feel like a "pitch".]

"He had read one of Julian Gomez's newsletters called the *Arbitrage Side Hustle,* which you can do in your spare time". —

[SOLUTION = PRODUCT]

"And it was working for him". —

[Proof]

"I was inspired by his success and I thought, well, **maybe this will be the thing that works for me too**" —

[The exact thought the writer wants to make the reader think.]

"So, I jumped in with both feet" —

[Pivot.]

"I was determined to make this work. The first three days I put in like sixteen hours a day". —

[Hard work here! But, wait for it…]

"I worked really, really hard, but by day 10 I had reached my freedom goal" —

[BOOM! Pivots into "FREEDOM GOAL"—the reader "fills in the gap" and comes to his own conclusion with his own "freedom goal"]

"And by day thirty, I was making $400 to $1,000 a day".—

[Fast, Easy, and Big]

"Sometimes even more than that, and now even two years

later…"—

[Stretch out benefits in time.]

"I'm only putting in a couple hours a day, but my life is so much more relaxed". —

[Easy + Desired result]

"My husband and I are doing so many **more of the things, we really want to do**. We both love to **travel**…" —

[Hits the nail on the head. Completely identifies with the prospect's desires.]

"And earlier this year, we **took a trip to Asia** with one of our **kids**". —

[Spending time with kids—that's exactly what the prospect wants.]

"I just returned from **Clearwater Beach Florida** where I spent time with my **daughters**". —

[Hammers the point home.]

"It was so fun on the beach in the sand, the sun, and dang it… I'm starting to peel from that already, but it was such a good time". —

[Great use of imagery—future pacing, painting the picture for the reader.]

"So, whatever you would do with your **spare money**, whatever your financial goals are…" —

[Knows reader has a "nest egg" to invest.]

"**If** you have even an ounce of determination, **you** can do this". —

["If…Then"—inclusion statement + gives reader belief in himself. Of course, they have an OUNCE of discipline.]

"My son, Trevor and I, are just two of hundreds of people who are making a living doing this, and you can too". —

[Social proof + hope]

"**I didn't invest a single dollar**, but I did invest my time and I am so glad that I did…" —

[The sucker punch! Overcomes the money objection and knows reader has a lot of spare time"]

Can you see that? Every single sentence was furthering the sale. Another reason why storytelling is so effective is because it lets the prospect decide for themselves and come to their own conclusion. This really is the greatest way of influencing someone. It's selling without selling. It prompts less resistance because it's so indirect.

Stories mold perception and touch the unconscious mind, which means you can reframe their perspective and overcome objections.

You know we spoke about the importance of proof earlier? Well, stories provide proof for the emotional brain. As you can see in the previous example (transcript), the writer adopted the reader's terminology to further identify with the prospect. Here's an example to illustrate the fact that everyone is telling themselves a different story.

Let's say there's two ten-year-old kids, Johnny and Jack. Every time Johnny loses, he throws a strop (he believes losing is a **bad thing**). Every time Jack loses, he becomes more intrigued (he believes losing is **feedback** for next time).

They both experience the same event (losing) but have different stories they're telling themselves.

If you can show this in your copy through a **character**, you're onto something. But you really need to know your reader inside and out. Because if you can't include the experiences and events the reader has experienced in the past, the story will bomb.

When using stories make sure you 'SHOW, don't TELL'.

SHOW: *"They squeezed each other, and the tweed of his jacket was rough under her cheek. His large hand came up to stroke her red hair; she smelled leather and horses on the skin of his wrist. He was trembling".*

TELL: *"They stood close and wrapped their long arms round each other in a passionate embrace, so that she became aware that he had been riding, and then that he was as nervous as she was".*

"Showing" paints the picture (mental movie) in the prospect's mind's eye, whereas telling is plain and boring. As you'll soon find out, painting pictures in your reader's mind is essential if you want to create a windfall of cash.

3 Elements That Evoke Emotion in Stories

- Identifies with the reader.

- The reader has had a very similar experience and can totally relate (visualizing the experience they've had).

- Implied call to action.

If the reader has had a similar **experience**, the **story** will start to replay in their mind and evoke an emotional response (anger and envy). You don't have to be the next Stephen King to persuade your prospect. A few sentences can do the job. In fact, you need to be more like a brain surgeon and pick inside your prospect's brain.

Let's say you're writing to the "typical" 9-5 worker that wants to quit his job. Here's an example of a short story:

"I worked my butt off and increased the business revenue by 40%, yet Alex just focused on the office politics and sucking up to the boss. He came out with a raise, and I didn't.
(READER HAD A SIMILAR EXPERIENCE)

I was doing more than double what Alex was doing. Closed twice the amount of deals and completed 200 more phone calls. I worked 2 hours overtime every single day, yet Alex was twiddling his thumbs behind his desk. He was just sweet talking every living soul that passed him by.
(IDENTIFY WITH THE READER)

And that's when I had enough. I was sick and tired of working for "the man" and building his empire. That's when I went to Dane to learn copywriting.
(IMPLIED CALL TO ACTION)

Listen, I keep my promises. Remember we were talking about how demonstration is the best form of selling, but in copy we can't physically demonstrate it? Well, let's talk about it.

Here are some ways you can demonstrate your product:
Marketers often use the $1 trial and very low dollar offers like (free + shipping). This way, you can let the prospect experience the product and see if he likes it. By the way, this is old as anything, but works so well. Why do you think everyone leads with free? Free gym trial, free cakes, free samples galore.

Stories That Demonstrate: Before I show you an example, read this with laser-like focus:

We feel and act according to what we believe or **imagine** to be true. In other words, we react to the mental images. And the best part, your nervous system cannot tell the difference between an **imagined** experience or a **real** experience. Make these pictures as vivid and real as possible.

Here is a story that demonstrates (short testimonial story):

Customer Quote: [PROBLEM] "I loved going to the gym but the one thing I couldn't stand is [OBJECTIONS] being tied into a contract and paying the pointless joining fee".

(Identifies with the prospect, uses exact same language + covers objection)

[SOLUTION] At this gym, you can get a monthly membership without paying a joining fee, with all classes included and best of all… You can cancel whenever you like at no extra cost.

Formula: [PROBLEM] + [OBJECTIONS] + [SOLUTION]

Stories that demonstrate achieve two things:

1—Increase desire.

2—Prospects "close" themselves (after "experiencing" a demonstration story and the results they'll get). It has the same effect as a takeaway close. I'll explain the "takeaway close" in more detail soon.

This can be very effective when it's used throughout the copy— they will experience or see the mental movie of owning the product. Let's say you had five short demonstration stories that hammered the same point. Each time you tell one and then transition to an unrelated point, the experience is taken away from them. It's kind of like having a juicy treat and teasing the dog repeatedly by putting the treat near his mouth, and yanking it back until he starts to salivate all over the floor. Pretty brutal.

The key: Know your prospect inside and out. Know the exact words they use when expressing objections or concerns and then feed it back to them. As mentioned before, here are a few ways:

- Talk to prospects.
- Talk to customers.
- If you have salespeople, talk to them.

- If you have customer service people, ask them about the most common questions and complaints.
- Look on sites like Amazon where there are reviews.

Elements of the Demonstration Story

- It was like this before
- It's like this now
- This is much better than it was

The Hero's Journey

1. The prospect is the **hero** (identify with the reader)
2. The product / service is the **guide** (product is the solution)
3. It's going to be a story about **transformation** (example, broke to rich)

Here's the Formula:

1. I had this problem
2. I looked for / tried everything as a solution
3. Nothing worked
4. I was about to give up
5. Then I discovered [product / service]
6. I used [the product / service]; here's what happened.

It might be easier and better in third person (currently better for ad network compliance as well). Here's an example in action:

Jon was always working two different jobs and struggling to make ends meet. Trading physical labor for dollars was draining him. He had no time or energy to spend with his loved ones.
[Problem]

He tried no money down in real estate, forex trading, and even Amazon dropshipping. After a few months, he tried starting up a social media marketing agency, and that failed as well.
[He tried everything]

After buying loads of courses and books on every possible business venture he attempted, he really felt as though he had nothing left. He tried calling people, going to seminars, and networking with people.
[**Nothing worked**]

After fourteen hours of hard labor every day and sacrificing his weekends for business ventures, he was about to throw in the towel.
[**He was about to give up**]

One night, he decided to go the corner shop to buy two bottles of Jack Daniels Whiskey. When he returned, he started searching the internet aimlessly... And somehow happened to come across *The Ultimate Copywriting System*.
[**Then he discovered product / service**]

He took the plunge and bought the course on a monthly payment option. After just three months, he quit both his jobs and is now earning $10,000 on average per month.
[**He used the product; here's what happened**]

When writing copy, use demonstration stories like salt and pepper. They don't need to be very long, but they're effective. On the other hand, if you want to include a sales hero journey story, use it like hot sauce. Only use it when it's necessary and when done properly it will set a fire in their belly.

5. Testimonials

We've already covered testimonials in depth beforehand. Here I'll give you some important points and examples: You don't need to leave testimonials till the end of the sales letter, either. Feel free to sprinkle them in, when the time is right.

Let's dissect this testimonial:

Others, like Kevin Shannon, have been able to put their kids through college...

"I have been following you for over a year your insights have been right on. You have helped me fund my children's education and also helped me pay some bills!"

—*Kevin Shannon*

"I have been following you for over a year (*social proof*). Your insights have been right on (*safety*). You have helped me fund my children's education (*major benefit + identify with readers desire*) and helped me pay some bills (*smaller benefit*) - Kevin Shannon (*little specificity*)"

It's got all the elements. Maybe could've done with a bit more specificity by adding in the location, for example, "Kevin Shannon, Houston, Texas"

Basic elements of a testimonial:

- Identify with reader
- One major + smaller benefit
- Specific
- Concise
- Paint picture (future pace)

6. Bullets: "Even if...", "Without..."

I will get into more depth about bullets later, but here's an easy way you can overcome objections in bullets. You can do it indirectly by saying something like, "How to earn up to $1000 per month by investing as little as a $100 bill" —that clearly covers the objection of money.

If you want something more formulaic—you can use words like "Even if..." and "Without". See this example:

> ✓ **How to claim a $152 Hanukkah check – even if you aren't Jewish.** It isn't common knowledge but the largest producer of Christmas toys was founded by a family with Jewish origins and gives back millions of dollars to those in the know each year. Page 49 explains how to be included in their beneficence. Mazel tov!

7. Guarantee

Objection: Money— *"If you don't make at least $200 in the first week, send us an email and we will give you a full money back guarantee"*.

Objection: Time— *"If you don't receive the book in the next 5 days, send us an email, and we will provide a full refund, plus we will send you a free audio version of the book, while the hardcopy is on its way"*.

8. FAQ's

This is a great way to overcome objections for a few reasons. There are certain readers that will skip all the way to the bottom to see what's on offer. These FAQ's will overcome most of their objections immediately. At the same time, the reader that read the entire sales letter might still have some concerns before taking action. This will help tip him over the edge.

As always, it needs to be in logical order. As you can see in this example, the first frequently asked question is the most obvious and logical one. Because after the writer has written about fifteen to twenty pages of copy for a free book, the first objection the reader will have "Is this really free? What's the catch?" All of this again shows the importance of knowing your market and the objections they raise.

9. In the offer

So far, we've covered eight ways to overcome objections within the actually copy itself. Let me preface: These next four paragraphs mostly apply if you're selling **information products** and looking to **release a new offer** (keep this in mind for your upcoming offers).

GOOD NEWS

There's an entire book on creating jaw dropping offers. Offers which make people line up begging for your product. You can get my book *The No-Brainer Offer* at:
https://daneknightonbook.com/the-no-brainer-offer/

If you already have an existing offer don't worry... I'll show you another way to overcome objections in just a second. But first, follow me closely here:

Instead of thinking of ways to overcome objections in the body copy, what if you removed those objections from the new offer altogether? For example, let's say you want to sell a digital course in the business opportunity niche. What if instead of asking customers to go through all the troubles of starting a complicated business... you showed them the quickest and easiest way to $10,000. Just for a moment, imagine you have the option of selling either one of these **info products**. Would you sell a digital course that teaches:

1. How to start a restaurant (which will have tons of hurdles in the way). The likes of small margins, importing food, volatility issues, hiring staff and petty regulations?

2. Or... would you sell a copywriting course where you would only need to teach them how to write copy and how to get clients?

Don't you think the second option is more appealing than going through all the struggles of starting a restaurant? I think so! You see, most people don't think about this when creating offers. People want the fastest and easiest way to get the results they want. But the more hurdles your offer has, the less sales you're going to make. In the offer, there are three different buckets where objections may arise. The vehicle, internal hang ups and external beliefs.

Vehicle: This is where the objection is based on the core product. It's the "thing" that gets the prospect to their desired end result. For example: let's say that you want the lifestyle where you can travel the world. To achieve this goal, you could do Amazon dropshipping, online coaching or copywriting. These are all just "vehicles" and your job is to make them believe in your "vehicle".

Vehicle Beliefs: (Core product—Copywriting Course for Online Business Owners)

This is where you get the prospect to believe the **only** way to achieve his desired end result is through the specific vehicle. For example, if he wants to run a successful business without hiring three-hundred telesales people, you need to show him that **copywriting** is the solution through every possible angle. The way you get him to believe this, is through the chain of logical reasoning.

Internal Beliefs: Here's where the prospect will have internal hang-ups and self-limiting beliefs about his own ability. Oftentimes, this is what stops most prospects from taking action. Your job as a copywriter is to give them hope and belief in themselves that they can do it, that it's possible. To overcome these internal beliefs, you could tell stories (3rd person testimonial or personal) which identifies with your target prospect and their current situation. That way, the prospect sees other people have been in the exact same position and have achieved the result they want.

You can also add <u>bonuses</u> to your **existing offers** to overcome some of these false internal beliefs. If the internal belief was "I understand copy is 80% of the success of the funnel, but I don't have the talent for writing and my grammar sucks". You can give away a free bonus that shows them *"How to Outsource All the Proof Reading and Editing for $50 a month"* —BOOM! The objection is obliterated.

External Beliefs: Take this objection: "I think I could write copy, but I don't know if it's good or not before I publish it". If that's the case, we can add Bonus #2: *"Get One Free Review Each Month from an A-List Copywriter"*.

By doing this, you suffocate all the objections and leave no room for the prospect to question anything else. Bonuses are versatile as they increase the value of the offer and overcome objections. But... don't get ahead of yourself! Here are two main elements of effective bonuses.

1. Very relevant – to the core product

2. Few – don't stack bonuses for the sake of it.

Let's say we have the common objection: "I don't have **time** to read the book". All you need to do is send them an audiobook. This automatically overcomes the objection, because everyone has to "commute" from one place to another during the day, and during this **time**, they can consume the product. There you go, that's how to overcome objections before you write any copy. Pretty cool, huh?

HOW TO USE THE HIDDEN SECRETS THAT ARE ONLY SEEN BY THE TRAINED EYE

Y ou must communicate these emotions throughout. Feel free to use a checklist of some sort.

Now, listen to me here: It's communicating, not directly stating. Instead of directly saying "this is new!" or "this is safe", you imply this through the communication with the deeper structure, not the surface level stuff. I'll show you few examples.

1. Novelty

When you tell people **NEW** things, it creates a dopamine spike in their brain, which can literally make your copy addictive. Because once they get a hit of dopamine, they want more of it. Give them new facts and information!

> And that's not fair.
>
> Because we've never seen anything like this historic boom... and never will again.
>
> **This is the EASIEST way to get rich you'll ever see.**
>
> And if you miss out, you'll regret it for the rest of your life.

> That's why I can't emphasize this enough... there's no time to waste...
>
> We will NEVER see an opportunity even remotely like this again in our lifetime.

> There's never been ANYTHING like this before...
>
> This is the true "get rich quick" opportunity you've spent your whole life waiting for...

All three of these examples are included in the same promotion, literally separated by a few sentences. Once you know what to look for, you'll see this communicated all throughout. When you first read copy, it just looks like "normal" general text. Now, it's much more than that; you can see what's really happening. Remember, every single sentence is furthering the sale. Not once did the writer say, "this is NEW". He communicated the fact, without using the exact words.

2. Security

"Playbook" + "step-by-step" implies that he will take the reader by the hand and show him the way. He doesn't have to do any hard work or create anything new.

"I've seen it happen to dozens of folks already"—That's social proof + safety. If others have already achieved the desired end result, it seems secure. In all three of these examples, never did the writer outright say "this is secure". You're now communicating with the deeper structure.

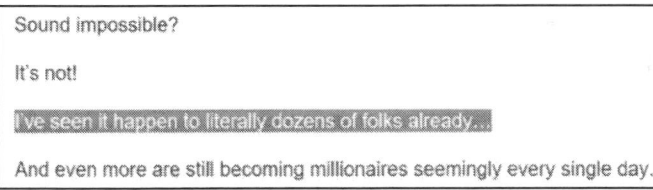

3. Greed: Fast + Easy + Simple + Large + Reframe

> These are NOT annual gains.
>
> These are NOT monthly gains.
>
> They aren't even weekly gains!
>
> These are gains that happened in a SINGLE DAY!

> Had you put $100 in when shares were trading for just pocket change...
>
> You could have turned your $100 stake into a quick $13,700 windfall.
>
> Invest $1,000 and you'd be looking at **$137,000 in profits!**

If you've been paying careful attention, you'll notice that most of these examples use large numbers (claims). To really tap into those greed glands, use **REFRAMING** ($100 - $1,000 – see below).

> Had you invested just $100 in each of those, you'd have walked away with a total of $77,041...
>
> All in around 24 hours each!
>
> Invest a little more, say $1,000...

4. Only

You must make the product the holy grail. The only way the prospect can get the result they desire, is through your product. And the only way to get it, is through this sales page.

Think back to the unique mechanism. It's the number one factor that communicates "ONLY". If you don't do this throughout the copy, the prospect will simply... Google the information you told him about and buy it from someone else.

For example, let's say you were selling a fitness supplement. If you had to say throughout the sales letter that branch chain amino acids are the "secret" ingredient to 25" arms. All the prospect will do is Google "branch chain amino acids" and buy them from another business. See what I mean here? You must make the sales page and the guru or personality the **only** place the prospect can get the product from. Let's look at another example of communicating "only":

Russell Brunson, an internet marketer, owns a software company called ClickFunnels. Basically, it's a software that allows you to build marketing funnels much faster than ever before. Think of it as a page builder. Here's how Russell communicates that the **only** way the prospect can achieve their desired end result is through ClickFunnels. Bear in mind, there are tons of other software services people can use.

Throughout his messaging—in his books, webinars, speeches, and events—he always talks about "funnels". You'll hear him say, "You're one funnel away…" from striking it rich. But he doesn't stop there… He makes prospects believe that ClickFunnels is the **only** way they can achieve this. All his front-end "marketing materials" like his books, are sales letters for his core flagship product (ClickFunnels). He makes ClickFunnels larger than life. Another example is Pot Stocks Sales Letter:

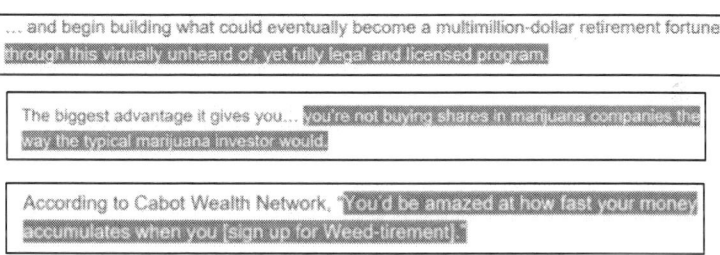

Basically, this sales letter talks about Marijuana Stocks. You can buy these stocks anytime you want. However, the writer uses neologizing by keying the term "weed-retirement" and positions it as a very low-risk option, because **he will show you** everything step-by-step.

Listen: Never, ever, finish a sales letter without communicating the **ONLY way to get the product is through the sales letter.**

In a nutshell, you communicate this through:

- Unique mechanism
- New "this is the first ever book of its kind. No one has seen anything like this"
- Neologizing (coining new words)

In other words, communicating these five critical factors is all about the underlying emotions that you spark, not the actual words you use.

NOT FOR THE WEAK MARKETER!

If you'd like to learn about the other 3 components that make the Unique Mechanism work, and you want to finally stand out and get more customers no matter how competitive your niche, I'd recommend you consult my book *The Unpublished Chapters*. It's the follow up book from the one you're reading right now. You can get this ADVANCED version at: https://daneknightonbook.com/the-unpublished-chapters/

WHAT YOU'RE REALLY SELLING

A ll copywriters have heard the good ol' saying "sell the benefits, not the features". While that's not entirely wrong, it's not the most effective, either.

The C-level Copywriters will pile benefit on benefit. They'll tell you what the product does for you, until you're blue in the face. Let me quickly cover the basics. Here's an example:

> **Features:** What the thing is (facts) "Red Ferrari"
> **Benefits:** What the product does for you "Red Ferrari attracts more attention".

See, that is very basic stuff and isn't going to sell million or even billions of products on its own. As we've discussed earlier, people don't buy the actual product; they buy something much more than that.

Now we need to - **Emotionalize the benefit:** Here's where we play the role of the narrator in the prospect's mental movie. You create this movie by painting pictures and showing the prospect all the ways he will enjoy the benefits. Here's an example:

"*Just imagine the next time you drive into town to take your date to the new restaurant that just opened. When you pull up to the red traffic light, the people walking on the footpath, the people in shops, and even the people in the other cars, stare at you in awe*".

This is what you want to concentrate on when someone says sell the "**benefits**"! If you can recall, I told you earlier that to change someone's beliefs, you must give them a **new experience** that creates a **new perspective**. This could either be a real-life experience or internal mental movie. That right there was an example of the "internal mental movie". Back to my point...

You need to make the prospect **feel** a certain way. Sell the **meaning** of the thing! Don't just sell the functional benefits: red color will attract attention and engine will increase speed. No, no! Instead, sell him on what life would look like AFTER. Make him envision the new experiences and emotions he will feel.

Look here: People don't buy a Ferrari for transportation and practical purposes. They buy power and recognition.

People buy things:

1. To make them feel better about themselves.

2. Move them away from pain.

3. Show others and remind themselves who they are.

It all comes down to social status. The pleasure that you derive from this Ferrari is all based on emotions. You're buying emotions and the metal frame is just a deliverable. An easy way to tap into the deeper emotions, is the "So what..." test.

Feature: Red Ferrari - So, what?

Benefit: It attracts attention - So, what?

Dimensionalize benefit: Next time you pull up at the traffic lights, all the people will stare at you in awe—BOOM!

That's why he really buys, for (**power**). He wants to feel dominant.

What you're really selling is...

Feelings and Identities. [PLEASURE! CONFIDENCE!

Instead of the "So what approach…" you can use: "And that means…".

FEATURE—Make *$20,000*.

BENEFIT—And that means you'll be able to go to any restaurant *without looking at price*.

FEELINGS—Which means you won't *FEEL* embarrassed when taking another person on a date.

IDENTITY—And that means you'll be a much more *powerful* and confident person.

Now you can smile knowing that we have officially reached the real reason why people buy. Before I carry on and **continue-continue,** I want to ask you something. But listen - I'm at an unfair advantage. Because as you'll soon see, I'm using some secret persuasion triggers right here. There's probably not much point me even using them. That means I'm forced to rely on the one and only persuasion technique I have left in my bag. The old fashioned - genuine request. What's the favor? Well, I need you to purchase 250 copies of this book to give to your friends, family members and business partners. No, I'm just playing with you. The favor is a small one. Even better you can choose between either one of them. If you want to do both even better! If you think this information has been helpful so far, you could help me a ton if you could:

- Take a picture with this book and post it on your social media (because it will help me market the book through social proof)

- Go to www.daneknightonbook.com/affiliate/ (which will help you earn a good chunk of cash without selling your own product)

After all, I would be setting a bad example… if I didn't use the same techniques I'm teaching, right? Okay let's keep going…

A cleaning company is not just selling a cleaner home. Instead, they sell the owner—**recognition** from their friends and family when they come to visit. At the same time, they're curing the pain of **embarrassment**. The homeowners don't want anyone to see their home in a dirty state. You can either...

Directly address the emotion: "You never have to feel depressed and ashamed that the women aren't attracted to you". Unless you've got a lot of trust built up, and the audience knows you, I wouldn't recommend this approach. It will prompt a lot of resistance and come across as rude.

Indirectly address the emotion: You can communicate this through the product benefits. For instance, look at the second line: The writer didn't say, "you're likely going to pass away soon, so it's best if you take your chance now". Instead, he communicated it subtly. Remember, the reader is retired and about seventy-years old.

> But you will NEVER see an easier way to get rich than explosive marijuana stocks... not in your lifetime.

Wouldn't you like a reliable *body copy formula* that you can use as a "go to"? Sure, you would! Here it is:

Objection + Claim + Proof (2-5 various forms) + Benefit

If you look at Agora Financial sales letters, they will have this formula in their body copy. In this example: Objections (first three sentences), Claim (fourth sentence), Proof (sixth sentence) Look:

> And the beauty is these buyouts happen no matter what's happening in the market...
>
> It doesn't matter if the company is in dire straits...
>
> Or if the economy as a whole takes a plunge.
>
> With help from this proprietary indicator, you don't even have to worry about a stock market crash.
>
> For example...
>
> When multi-billion dollar insurance company, XL Group entered the Buyout Zone on March 1st...
>
> XL Group Ltd (XL)

If you've read any other copywriting books, they'll always tell you to pile on the benefits. But…What do you do when you don't have any tangible benefits? Like writing a promo for a charity donation.

There's only one answer and it's been working for the longest time: You stimulate powerful emotions the target prospect has **already** boiling up inside them. You see, people who donate to fundraising projects, do so all because of emotions. Maybe it's guilt. Maybe it's for benevolence. It's all emotions, and there's no way around it. They get nothing tangible back in return.

It goes back to the old Robert Collier principle (start with the conversation going on in the reader's mind). It's like a river. Why would you want to be a salmon swimming upstream against the tide when you can flow with the tide?

So, how do you apply this?

Start with a clear understanding of the prospect's state of mind and how he **already feels** about the subject. You do not start with the product and its benefits. That's starting ass backwards.

Start with the prospect's core emotions and then only craft the sales message around these already boiling emotions. Add an underlying emotion to every piece of copy, whether it's the offer, call to action, headline… everything. Leave no stone unturned.

If everyone buys on emotion, doesn't it make sense to hammer it repeatedly? I thought so! But appealing to emotion alone will only get you so far. You need to give the prospect the logical excuse to purchase the product. So, here's what you do:

Start with the *PRODUCT* when you want to appeal to Logic— Benefits, Benefits, Benefits.

Start with the *PROSPECT* when you want to appeal to Emotion— Emotion, Emotion.

How to Identify the Emotions?

1. Theatre of the mind

Close your eyes and imagine the prospect's typical day. What emotions would they feel?

For example, a male teenager that is suffering from severe acne. What emotion would he feel when he wakes up every day with a new pimple and there's almost nothing that he can do about it? (**frustration**). And every time he leaves his house to go out in public, he will experience (**embarrassment**). When he is close-up, talking to other people, he will feel (**insecure**). How do I know this? Simple. That was my story.

2. Talk to family and friends—see what emotions are dominant.

3. Talk to other people in the target market: Immerse yourself in their world; read what they read (magazines, books), watch what they watch. Basically, consume all the information they're consuming. This will help get in touch with what the prospect thinks, feels, and believes.

All target markets will have different psychographics. Take the automobile industry as an example. Rolls Royce and Toyota both sell cars. But their target market has completely different criteria. One is buying prestige and power, while the other is buying transportation. One is more concerned with practicality than recognition. Volvo appeals to buyers that value security.

4. Ask customers (open ended questions).

5. Ask angry customers (they will let all their emotions out)—Use Amazon Reviews 5 Star and 1 Star.

6. Look at what works for your competitors and what they're testing.

7. Forums—Quora, Reddit and others.

This might sound obvious, but instead of looking at the features and benefits of the product and spewing them all over the page, look at the features and benefits the readers care about - and write about the sales points that will motivate them to buy.

What's the point of telling them about 400-horsepower when they only care about the safety of the vehicle? You'll lose them immediately.

Before you write any promotion, I highly suggest you find out your prospect's "Core Emotional Complex". Find out their beliefs, feelings, and desires. Let's use the Agora Financial customer avatar as an example (this is a rough guideline) —

Beliefs: They believe that the folks on Wall Street are hiding something from them, and keeping all the secrets for themselves.

Feelings: Primary emotion is fear of dying, losing a partner, and leaving the family with a financial burden. They may also experience embarrassment in certain situations, especially related to loved ones. They might not be able to take their loved ones on vacation, whereas their next-door neighbors do so all the time.

Desires: They want to find a good investment vehicle that will allow them to travel the world and have great experiences. Live a life without worrying too much about finances and leave resources for their loved ones when they pass. Their main desires are more related to noble causes like giving to charities and family. They would like to experience as much as they can… in the time they have left.

EVERYONE BUYS ON EMOTION, HERE'S HOW TO STIMULATE IT

Let's get back to emotion. You need to provoke emotion to get people in a buying mood. If you want to get an overweight person to sign up for a personal training service or any related
weight loss product, you could ask them the following:
*"How would you **feel** if you gained another ten pounds year after a year? How would your partner **feel** and think when you've gained another ten pounds? At the moment, she is only looking at*

*men, but soon that may change to something different. And what about your kids? How would you **feel** when you aren't able to play sports with them?".*

That right there is stirring the emotions. It's not telling her about all the benefits of the product, like: this has X ingredient and this has Y ingredient.

Think about it for a moment, and I'm sure you'll agree: The vast majority of the money that flows through our hands each year is spent to meet our emotional needs—NOT to satisfy our need for physical survival. We can physically survive if we have air, water, calories, and shelter. You can get the first two free. Calories and shelter won't put you out of pocket, either. All the other money that is exchanged is spent to meet emotional needs: The craving for personal status, security, love, power and much more.

B-writers sell on plain benefits and logical reasons. By doing this, they're trying to justify the purchase and price of the product by appealing to the intellect alone. That's like going to a paintball game and leaving 99% of your paintballs in the locker! Rather than boring the prospect to death with plain jane benefits and reasons why they should purchase the product, you want to become a detective and address the already existing powerful emotions.

These are the ones that move the prospect closer to taking action on the offer. Emotions will mix together and they're very closely related. You want to pull at the heart strings and then push. Pull the emotional string of fear (being poor and going broke), then at the same time, push the button of greed (making tons of money) and being able to do whatever you want (power). Combine the "push" emotions with the "pull" emotions and 1+1=3. Here are some emotions worth stirring:

ANGER: This is one of the best emotions you can trigger. Do this correctly and you can really get the prospects blood boiling. When using anger, you must use a "target". An enemy— *"Those Wall Street Insiders have been hiding this information from you all along".* Anger is derived from a sense of injustice, unfairness, or unmet expectations. Think back to the time when someone cut you off in traffic.

Or maybe your partner cheated on you (broke your expectations). The root cause comes from **the way he thinks things should be**. Anything different that happens, is bound to cause anger.

BETRAYAL: It's a form of anger. Betrayal is a form of deception and happens because people feel they have been intentionally deceived, and had their trust shattered. Whether it's a partner cheating on you, or a business partner lying about something, being intentionally deceived like this will definitely lead to a feeling of betrayal.

REVENGE: Show the prospect how he is being abused or deceived and prove the problem is real, then present the solution against the enemy [product] and highlight how he will be fighting back against them.

FEAR: It's a very dominant emotion in health and investment. It cannot be used alone; it needs to work together with greed to be effective. Like Yin and Yang.

Great copywriters will use the fear of loss and then immediately present the greed of gain. That way, the prospect still associates the product for what it gives him!

FRUSTRATION: Find out what your prospect is frustrated with and position your product or service as the solution. This works great in highly sophisticated markets where everybody is saying the same thing.

FORBIDDEN: It's a primal emotion. Strike this one at its core and you're onto something. Agora uses this one all the time.
For example, *"The rich folks at Wall Street don't want you to see what goes on behind closed doors"*.

GREED: Very effective in selling. It's not always about money; instead, it's more of anything. To really maximize the effectiveness of greed, partner it with maximum credibility and vivid imagery. People are more likely to act when they can see themselves experiencing the end result in their own mental movie.

HOPE: Make the guru more credible and believable. Testimonials are also great (the reader will identify with other people just like him that have been through his struggles). Provide loads of proof.

LOVE: The most effective way to use this is in combination with fear, such as the threat or possibility of something happening to a loved one. Then, position your product as the solution to prevent this from happening; *"Make sure you and your loved ones always have sufficient income"*.

PASSION: Most great testimonials are passionate and believable.

POWERLESNESS: *"You can surrender to those who have almost destroyed your wealth"*.

RELAX: Paint vivid pictures in your prospect's mental movie. They will associate the words and images with the product or service.

SADNESS: Not as frequently used as fear or anger. Typically, sadness is less actionable. Think about it: When's the last time you were sad and decided to take massive action? Almost never.

When to use it:

When your prospect is in a depressed or low state, use this to create a contrast to the place he is currently in (or about to enter) to the very positive place he will find himself after purchasing and using the product. This contrast makes the benefits more appealing. Used in testimonials (from depressed state to happy state) "before and after" stories. You can use this emotion as a bridge to more actionable motivators like fear, anger, and revenge.

SECURITY: The massive dominant emotion in financial promotions. Security is the antidote of fear. The more secure someone feels, the less fear they experience. It's the emotion that provides **risk relief**. Use this emotion particularly in the close section of the sales message [order form and guarantee]. A lot of this emotion is used in the proof or credibility section of the copy. It makes the reader feel **safe** (he will now trust you). Use this and the resistance of the prospect will crumble.

SHAME or EMBARASSMENT: This is one of my favorite motivators. Everyone has such as tendency to move away from shame (it's unbelievably primal). For example, take the case of a guy that has just been made redundant and as very little savings and two young kids. If he doesn't have much money to do fun stuff with the kids, he will most likely experience tons of shame, and this could affect other areas of his life, such as dating. Present a shameful experience that your prospect can identify with and then position the product as the relief to the shame.

SURPRISE: Another primal emotion. It's great for grabbing attention and maintaining it throughout the copy. This emotion is frequently used in headlines "Little-known", "Shocking"

URGENCY: Very, very effective and makes the prospect act now! Mostly used in the "close" section of the copy. But, to make it even more effective, use it sparingly in the body copy. It conveys importance!

BULLETS

> ✓ **Collect A Rare 7% GOLD Dividend** That NOBODY Is Talking
> About! (It's Paid Like Clockwork For Over 10 Years, Too!)
>
> ✓ How To Make **$35 An Hour Walking On The Beach... Earn
> Up To $1,720 In "Backdoor Rental Income"**... Go Shopping
> And NET CASH The Next Time You Go To The Grocery Store...
> And More!

Bullets are very popular in book promotions to "tease" the prospect about what he is about to receive. It's again... more foreplay. Bullets can be used all throughout the copy—after the headline, teaser envelope, front and back cover of books, and most commonly, in the body copy. Here are the elements of bullets:

- Stimulates curiosity and intrigue.
- Creates more interest and spices up copy.
- Grabs the reader's attention and keeps him reading the copy.
- Increase desire—making the prospect want to know **HOW** to get the result.

Most of the time, the bullet must make the prospect think, "How do I do this? You're basically telling them *WHAT* it is and *WHY* it's important without revealing the solution. These are more commonly known as blind bullets. There are a few things to keep in mind: Vary your bullets so the copy has a natural flow—don't bore the reader (he will skim over otherwise).

Use a mix of these and you'll be fine:

1. **Blind bullets:** They don't give away the solution.

> ✓ **A little-known Wall Street trick to boost your income by $759 per month!** One of Wall Street's best-kept secrets allows you to boost your monthly income by turning every stock in your portfolio into an income-gusher. (Page 119)

2. **Direct bullets:** Shows the prospect the solution, but still piques his curiosity. *"Build stronger bones by eating apples! Proven in university study"*.

3. **Long bullets** (more common)
4. **Short bullets**

The Elements of Good Bullets:

- ✓ Build Intrigue / curiosity.
- ✓ Specificity (more believable).
- ✓ Interesting random fact: eg "This hasn't stopped President Trump from taking advantage of it".
- ✓ Offers a benefit.
- ✓ Specific mechanism (increases believability).
- ✓ Proof & credibility (Trumps "Secret Ingredient").
- ✓ Colloquial expression (say a lot with fewer words).

Here's a simple bullet formula:

Benefit + explosive image in customers mind + covers objection.

You really want to use action verbs, power words, slang, and benefits. Let me break down one of Gary Bencivenga's bullets for his $5,000 seminar DVD's.

"The easiest way to apply the secrets of Warren Buffet, America's smartest investor, to the process of marketing and wind up far richer. Very few marketers have ever thought of this".

- ✓ **Intrigue and curiosity:** Makes me think, "What is Warren Buffet secret, and HOW can I apply this to my marketing?".

- ✓ **Credibility:** "Warren Buffet" and "America's smartest investor".

- ✓ **Interesting random fact:** Makes me think, "How can I apply investing secrets to marketing?" and "What are these secrets?" as "Very few marketers have ever thought of this".

- ✓ **Benefit:** Become far richer.

- ✓ **Specific mechanism:** Warren Buffet's Secrets.

The writer also communicates:

Easy - "The easiest way".

Novelty - "Secrets" + "very few marketers have ever thought of this".

Security - "Warren Buffet, America's smartest investor".

Fast - "The easiest way to apply these secrets…. And wind up far richer".

As you can see, there's a lot going on in just one bullet. But now you know what elements are included, it will be that much easier.

FUTURE PACING

A s we've already established, you're selling the result, not the features of the product. All future pacing means is getting the reader to see themselves in their mind's eye after purchasing the product.

You'll see words like these being used frequently: "Imagine", "Picture", "See". For example:
"Just imagine if you had an extra six figures piled into your retirement savings right now".

Three are many ways you can future pace:

1. Description of the product's **appearance** or the **result.**

> Just imagine finally breaking free from the financial shackles that've held you down for so long...
>
> Imagine what it would be like to wake up to reliable and consistent gains of $22,031, $50,400 and even $59,440 month in and out... forever...

2. Product in **action** description: **Show** how it works.

"The coffee mug will be flickering with all the rainbow colors while the caffeine rushes through your blood ".

3. Invite the reader into his new world: Give a **verbal demonstration.**

"Picture this. Next weekend, you go down to visit both of your sons at their homes; the same routine you've been following for years. You've made only one simple change to this routine, so easy that your sixteen-year-old son could do it. But now, when you go to that local Italian restaurant, there's a dramatic change.

You start to look at the menu differently. From the very first moment, you'll pay attention to the left side of the menu rather than the right side [the prices]. You'll feel a sense of relief and security. No longer do you have to worry about your retirement savings when taking your kids out".

4. Show him how to test the claims.

"When you get your first investment newsletter, here is all you do: Open your electronic device. Spare five minutes and go to xyz.com. Now, all you do is make two simple clicks on your mouse. Next, click done. And now you've bought your first stock".

5. Future benefits (continuous flow of benefits): Over a span of weeks and months.

"First, you'll be able to quit your job and fire your boss (BENEFIT 1). But this is just the beginning! Within one week you would've had at least a hundred sales on AUTOPILOT (BENEFIT 2). And then, you convert these prospects on monthly retainers of $5,000 per month (BENEFIT 3). And when your schedule becomes jam packed, you can increase your price to $10,000 per sales letter (BENEFIT 4). You will see money that you've never imagined before. You will be able to take your loved ones on mind blowing vacations (BENEFIT 5) and when your neighbors and friends see this, they'll be jealous as ever... (BENEFIT 6)".

6. Show experts approving.

"Just imagine Warren Buffet's reaction to this Return on Investment".

7. Show their dark side.

Expose them! Show the disadvantages of the old product and lay it side by side with the advantages of the new product.

*"While everyone else is paying **$29.97** for this book on Amazon, having to wait five days for shipping, and not receiving all the extra bonuses… readers of **this** page can get the exact same book for free".*

8. Paint a dark picture of the old and then transition to the new product.

"Fat tires on your bicycle means wasting time, wasting money, and makes your legs look weaker when those old ladies overtake you. Now look at the new thin tires—it eliminates the heavy feeling, gives you the full performance you deserve… and this is one of the toughest, strongest, longest-lasting tires ever made".

9. Show how easy it is to get these benefits.

"One week from today, you are going down to check your bank statement… And with just a few clicks of the mouse, and thirty seconds work, you could've locked in a massive $10,000 income check".

MAKING THEM BELIEVE

I f you've used just a few of these techniques I've been teaching you… The prospects will have their knees on the floor, begging for the product.

You've built desire to the tipping point and he is on a high. Now, you must maintain that high, and make him believe even further that he needs this product or service. Here are some ways to do this:

Inclusion Statements: You will see **"If… then"** statements being used more than anything else. They're crazy effective and there are a few reasons why. They act as a form of proof, mainly because you're speaking directly to the reader. You identify with the reader and he feels like you understand him. You can use an "If…then" statement in almost any claim and make it seem believable. That's why it's so effective. It adds believability. Look at these examples, and read them as they are, then re-read them without the "If…then" statements. Example:

*"**If** you're creative, **you** can get started with $0 and launch risk-free".*

Compare that with:

"You can get started with $0 and launch risk- free".

The first one is much more believable. Another reason why these inclusion statements are so effective, is due to logical reasoning and belief structures. I'll cover this in just a little while. It will make a lot more sense then. But for now, just know these statements lead to a cause and effect conclusion. Example:

*"**If** you earn more than $1,000,000 per month, **then** you're successful".* — It links two ideas together.

CONNECT-THE-DOTS THINKING

If you can get this working, you'll be able to skyrocket sales. See what I did there? Ah ha! Now you're learning. When I refer to "connect the dots" I'm talking about the underlying structure of the words. For example:

"The better the copywriter, the more sales you make. The more sales you make, the faster your business grows. And the faster your business grows, the more freedom you'll have".

I'll say it for the second time! The "secret" when using this technique, is to begin with the end in mind. You know, as a business owner, you ultimately want more freedom. But first, you need to grow your business. Now that you know that, you show the business owner how copywriting is the key to building his business. This logical structure gives the feeling of inevitability, because not only has he been told it works, he has been shown **proof** it works. It always goes back to the overarching principle—**the chain links of beliefs**. Copywriting to Sales > Sales to Business Growth > Business Growth to Freedom.

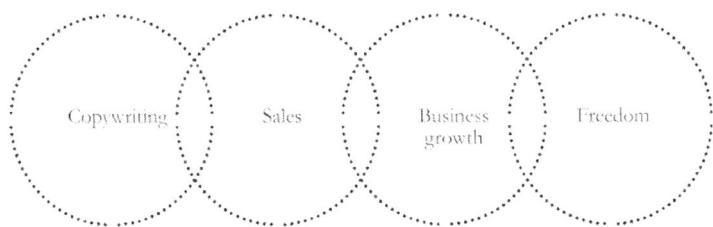

You start with the prospect's model of the world and all the beliefs and facts that he currently accepts as true. Once he has accepted the statements, you gradually and logically add one chain link to another until you get him to believe that he needs your product. You don't push the prospect to force his foot into a size 5 shoe, when he's a size 12. You get a shoe that fits his foot [model of the world] and then you can begin to persuade him. We're in the business of channeling and influencing beliefs.

REPETITION OF PROOF

Master persuaders use this persuasion technique all the time. You know the Martin Luther King speech, right? I lost count how many times he said "I have a dream". That wasn't for nothing though; this form of litany (repetition) builds intense desire and gives an element of proof. Take this example: Look at the sheer repetition of the words "They use".

*"**They use** these remedies to prevent infections. **They use** them to lower their cholesterol and protect their heart. **They use** them to get rid of aches, pains, and stiffness. And **they use** them to prevent strokes, Alzheimer's, and cancer"*.

You can also use this technique to stair step your way to a bigger claim—cough cough—**chain links of beliefs**. Here's what I mean:
    The writer couldn't have made the huge claim right outa the gate. *"They use these remedies to prevent strokes, Alzheimer's and cancer"*. The reader would be laughing his ass off with skepticism. If, however, he started like he did—with a smaller claim (which the reader already believes), then a larger one and then only the big claim of preventing cancer. It would be more readily accepted. While we're on the topic, let's talk more about repetition.

INTERNAL REPETITION

The mere use of repetition arouses desire and builds even more interest. The repetition tends to focus the prospect's attention on whatever is being communicated. Here's an example of repetition in action: That same phrase *"Single $100 bill"* was repeated **eight times** in one sales letter.

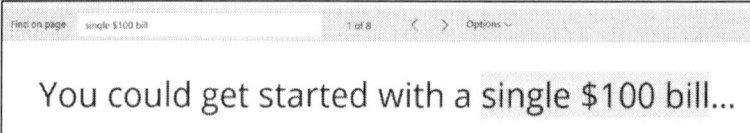

116

THE CLOSE

A t this point, you've got the reader hooked, and now you just need to close him. There are many techniques you can use. First, I want to address the main principles.

You can either make a:

Hard offer: Asking for money upfront

An example is a "direct sale" where you sell a product for $49 straight to cold traffic. Most of Agora's offers are straight sales. They write a mammoth 30-page sales letter to sell a $49 newsletter.

Soft offer: Billed later

This will attract tons more customers on the front-end, as it's so risk relieving. Just know, it may not be the highest quality customers. Examples: free trials, payment options, pay only after you've seen results. With a really great "soft offer" you can get away with sloppy copy. Creating an irresistible offer is the corner stone to a successful promotion. As they say… "you can't polish a turd".

The best copy in the world won't convert if:

(1) the Big Idea isn't good enough and (2) if the offer sucks.

Let's talk about the techniques that will make the cash register ring. Listen up, you don't need to use all of them. Sometimes one technique will make more sense than others, depending on many factors. There will be principles to follow that I will point out along the way. With that said, lets jump into it!

FALSE CLOSE

If you've ever watched the late-night TV commercials, you've probably heard the phrase "But wait there's more…". Although the phrase is a little worn out and fatigued, the concept works like gangbusters. The false close is where you add one more big benefit to push them over the edge, before asking for the dough. By the end of your sales letter, they really want the product, but might have some hesitations. The false close is the icing on the cake.

It's the benefit most writers don't think about, and done properly, the false close increases customer satisfaction because it sets a frame where they can expect to be surprised in the future. So, not only are you exceeding their expectations on the first sale, you're also laying the framework for a positive outcome on all future sales (increasing customer lifetime value). This will allow you to spend more to acquire a customer and scale your business to the moon.

In other words, A-list copywriters know the close is more than just making a single sale—they know that if you execute it right, you lay the foundation for many more sales in the future.

CREATE A HIGH PERCEIVED VALUE

1. Compare apples to oranges

Here you establish the normal price for one of your products or services, and then compare it to something different. Hence apples to oranges, not apples to apples. This technique will give the prospect a different perspective and a frame of reference to compare price. For example, let's say your **consulting fee** is $20,000 for 1 hour and the **course** you just released is only $997. If you came out and said the price is $997 without a point of reference for comparison, the price would seem quite steep. However, the fact that the prospect has accepted and knows your time is in effect worth $20,000 for one hour, it seems like a bargain.

Now, you tell the prospect how many hours it took you to make the course. Let's say twenty hours. So actually, the course is worth 20,000 x 20 = $400,000. That $997 seems like an absolute steal now. Make sure it's believable. Look at this example:

> I charge $2,000 for a 1-hour consultation.
>
> Please understand, this formula took me hundreds of hours to put together.
>
> But let's say it only took me 40 hours. If you multiply $2,000 times 40 you get $80,000.
>
> And to be fair...

2. Sell money at a discount (demonstrate ROI)

Show the buyer how the product pays for itself, how it's actually "FREE". Show the Return on Investment (ROI)—how much is **made** and **saved**, and how he is actually losing money right now as he reads this. If you can find a way to demonstrate this, you have the power of selling millions of products. You can also increase **believability** with an "Even if I'm 50% right, it will still make you x". For example:

"If I created a marketing funnel and charged you $10,000, but in one month you made $50,000 and every month after that, would it be worth $10,000? But let's say I only increased your revenue by (50%) $25,000, would it be worth it?".

"If the bank offered you $2.5 for every $1 you gave them, how often would you make the exchange? As many times as you could, right?".

Let's take this a step further. I've shown him how he can **make** money. Let's push him over the edge and show him how he is losing money day-by-day and can actually **save** more money.

"And get this... for every day that passes, you're in effect taking $1,666 and setting it on fire. In fact, you're actually losing a minimum of $5,000 per day because of all the missed back-end sales. Can you see how you're leaving so much money on the table every day by having a broken marketing funnel?"

Don't sell "products"; sell dollars for dollars. Instead of saying, this will "cost" you $50,000, you show the prospect how he gets an insane return on his investment. Like this:

"Would you give me $50,000 for a sales letter, if I increased your revenue from $100,000 per month to $250,000?".

3. Totaling the values

You give the "value" by simply telling him what you say it is.

☑ **One Year Subscription to *The Penny Stock Letter* –** You'll gain access to my very best money-making ideas... every month. Including instant text alerts when my emails hit your inbox; so you never miss a beat. **A $99 value - Yours for only $18.98!**

☑ **The Complete Penny Stock Course: Learn How To Generate Profits Consistently By Trading Penny Stocks. Sold on Amazon for $28.97. Yours for only $1!**

☑ **Retire Rich with Penny Stocks Video Series –** I'll personally walk you through all my secrets on camera. **A $599 value - Yours FREE!**

... And so, the **total value of everything you get today** adds up to **$726.97.**

And yet you can **have it all for only $19.98.**

This promotion has been running for a long time and I could only guess it's selling like hot cakes. One of the main reasons, I feel (in regard to the offer) is the **pre-established value** of the book on Amazon.com. The reader can clearly see it sells for **$28.97** and many people have already paid that amount. The reader thinks "I can have all this for only $19.98" and the book itself is worth $28.97. This is a no brainer!". Not only that, he is also getting all the other products as well! This is a great offer! But keep this in mind. The newsletters, the book, and the other bonuses will all be filled with sales copy. The book will be a disguised sales letter to sell more products. That's the reality, and that's how they will recover their front-end marketing costs.

Today ONLY...
Claim My Million-Dollar Blueprint For Just $1

I want to make sure you got the most out of this Million-Dollar Blueprint.

So, I have an incredibly generous offer to make you.

You see, this book retails on Amazon for $28.97. Take a look...

4. The liquidating bonus

If you can make this technique work, you really are onto something! Here's what you need to do:

1. First establish the price the customer is about to pay is a bargain (apples to oranges comparison).

2. Add the liquidating bonus as part of the false close.

3. Add the premium with an already established value that is equal to the product itself.

The example you're about to see is from Agora Financial. The product was being sold at $2,000; however, for the sake of this example, let's keep their "normal" price of $49.

You want to establish the total value is in excess of the product **(totaling the value) $5,000**. This makes the **$49 (product price)** seem like a steal. Take this example, the writer establishes a value of more than $5,000.

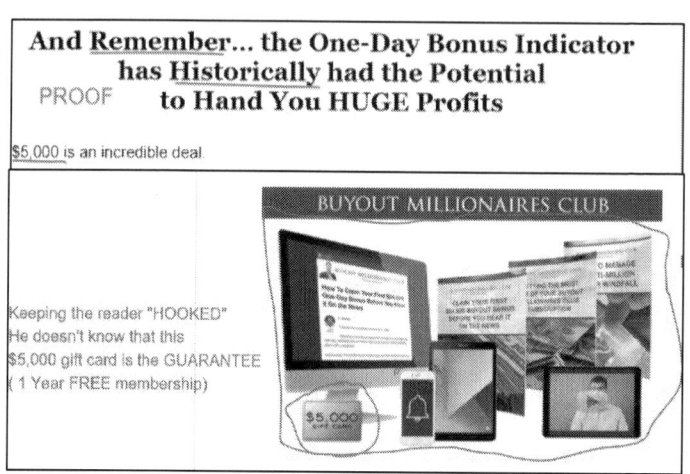

Now, you add a **premium bonus.** In this case, Agora is charging $49 for the newsletter, which means they need to find a product with an **already established retail value of at least $49.** In this case, they used a Samsung tablet.

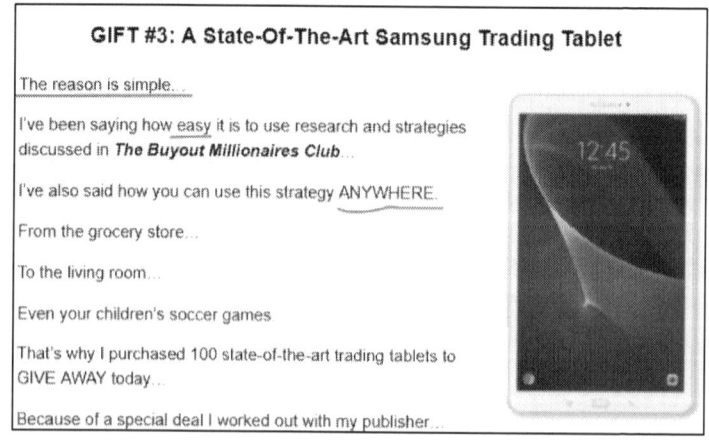

When the reader finds out the price, he will think: *"This is a no brainer! If I invest $49 today, I get a tablet worth as much as $100+. In fact, I actually make more money than I'm spending. All the rest of the bonuses are free!"*. And to add the cherry on top, you tell the customer to keep the premium bonus (Samsung Tablet) if he wants to cancel. That way, he really has nothing to lose and everything to gain.

The trick to making this work, is to find a product with a **pre-established retail value** that has been **severely discounted**. Also, it needs to be a product the reader would most likely be interested in and familiar with! You can try to import from China or maybe find a good deal from wholesale stores. The liquidating bonus is not something that you use all the time, but when you can, it's very powerful!

5. Sell bulk

List every single benefit of the product. For example, here you can see they listed every single ingredient. This increases the value and builds desire. This is particularly important when it comes to consumable products. Imagine if you had to sell an apple, and just described a few benefits. It would seem invaluable. But, if you described the benefit of each part of the apple like the skin, seeds, the color... it would appear more valuable. Look at the example: I know you can't read the text... but you get the principle.

6. Discuss the price paid / story

This goes back to the unspoken mechanism and story being told. Why do you think the Mona Lisa is worth millions while some painting in the streets of Mexico only sells for 3 bucks? The painter might very well be a lot better, but I doubt they're five million times better. One of the main reasons the Mona Lisa is so expensive, is the story behind it. Here's another example. See how he tells the story of discovering the "Unique Mechanism" and how it took him years plus $2.4 million. He of course, provided proof so the reader can believe it.

You see...

About 3 years ago...

Agora Financial started attracting attention from the top of Wall Street.　　Credibility

We were rapidly expanding...

And we met with some of the most elite traders and financial management teams on Earth...

In order to try and set up a brand-new research service focusing on mergers and acquisitions.

We met with many firms...

But one firm in particular was head and shoulders above the rest.

The firm which can only be identified as "F-1100345."

They had developed a proprietary trading software that was being leased out to multi-billion dollar hedge funds...

And you can take advantage of them all thanks to this $2.4 million deal I've signed with one world's most prestigious financial institutions...

Here's another example:

"This took me ten years of hard work travelling all over the world and spending $150,000 on courses and books. With over $175,000 spent to get this proven information in your hands, you can now have it for $14".

7. Present value vs price

This is like what we've discussed before, but with a slight twist. When doing this, you must provide believable **reasons why** the price is so low compared to the value. Again, you can do this by using (already established products).

Let me show you how to use this:

"If you were to go to other high-end seminars, you'd have to pay $35,000 dollars to get... just a tiny bit of info like this. Today, you have the chance to get one hour free with myself and Jay Abraham. Usually, Jay charges $20,000 for just 1 hour, and of course, you already know I charge $10,000 minimum. If you add all this up, it's $30,000 worth of value. But if you act today, as a bonus, you can get a one-hour hot seat from myself and Jay for only $2,997".

8. Full price example

This is very commonly used on free + shipping book offers to show the prospect he can **only** get this screaming bargain on the sales page. Just like the example I showed you earlier with the "penny stocks" book. *"If you go buy this book on Amazon it's $28.96, but on this page, you can get it for free".*

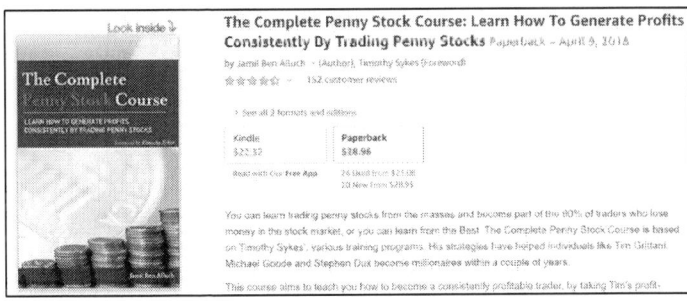

9. Reduction down to the ridiculous

Here's where you show them how much the product is per month, week, or per day. It makes the price seem less intimidating.

"The investment for this newsletter is $49".
"The investment for this newsletter is $0.13 per day".

10. Free relevant and complimentary bonuses

This is self-explanatory, however here's something to take home. You can use other people's products as bonuses for your core offer. I've seen this technique create crazy irresistible offers. This really works like gangbusters if you're selling information products, because there aren't any manufacturing costs involved. It also benefits both parties (the seller and the complimentary host). The seller gets to sell more products whereas the third party gets commission on each sale, and / or the opportunity to pitch them on the backend.

I've seen someone take their core offer and add an additional 10 (external joint venture) bonuses where each bonus has a **pre-established value** of at least $1,000. The customer then gets a value of $10,000, plus the actual core offer. Bear in mind, the prospects already knew and accepted the price point of each of those offers. If someone asked you for $2,000 cash and they gave you $12,000 cash in return, you'd jump on that offer right away, wouldn't you? Well that's exactly what happened! It was crazy!

11. Lead with a free bonus and then "sell" the core product at the end

To get the bonus, they have to get the product. It's kind of like telling your kids they can eat their favorite candy, but first they must eat their vegetables. Leading with the bonus is powerful because it also allows you to lead with free or a very low dollar offer. Like the previous example. They sold the book for $1 but the prospect needed to purchase the newsletter before he could get the book.

And Today You Can Claim My Entire Million-Dollar Blueprint ... For Just $1

That's right.

For the first time ever, my team and I compiled all of the details of my million-dollar secret into a new 385-page book.

And you can claim it for just $1.

12. Sell mystery and secrets

As you'll soon see, most people believe there are secrets and are always looking for the magic bullet. This is just the way we're wired. We want the path of least resistance. There are a few ways to inject some mystery into the copy. Using **unique language** and **terminology** will add more mystery, because the reader hasn't heard it before. The **unique mechanism** plays a massive role in adding mystery as well. Let me show you how powerful mystery is:

"I just wrote a $25,000 sales letter in one week and it's already made $100,000 as we speak. I used the "Hexagon" technique and literally just filled in the gaps. Not bad for a week's work, hey?".

Can you spot the technique I used to create mystery? It's **Neologizing** (coining a new name). The word "Hexagon" automatically sparks the readers curiosity. It's just a made-up phrase.

Another way is to differentiate: Use different packaging, price, and story. If you're selling a copywriting course, instead of selling it as an online course, wrap it up into something different that the reader hasn't ever seen.

13. Takeaway selling

Qualification: You're seen as more valuable if you're busy and the client must jump through hoops. Let's take an example. When a client wants to work with me as a copywriter, they must:

127

First, fill out an application form. If they qualify, my assistant will short-list them. After going through the short list, he will contact them for a call to see if it will be a good fit to work with each other. If the client seems like a good fit, my assistant will make the deal and then only will I speak to the client.

There's a reason why I make prospects go through this process. Number one, because it weeds out all the tire kickers. Number two, it's good positioning. The strong positioning also desensitizes price dramatically because when a business owner comes to me, they know that great copy is the best investment. You put $25K in and get $100K out. The client has to sell themselves to me. Let me tell you something: <u>people want what they can't have</u>.

Disqualification: This one is used very frequently, and with good reason. A popular phrase you may have heard "This is not for everybody". The trick to using this technique is really knowing your reader well. Because what you're really saying is, "this product is exactly for you, and nobody else". When you do this properly, the reader feels like you're talking directly to him. Look, this is a perfect example:

I'm Not Interested in Giving Away Free Books to Just Anyone

If you're the type who always says you want more out of life, but you never take action like you should... please don't request a free book.

If you're a habitual "starter"... but not really a "finisher"... not one grain of good will come from you holding *The Side Hustle Bible* in your hands.

We're looking for active, take-charge types who are eager to make good use of our hard work. Not those who will just let this book gather dust on their bookshelves.

Can you see how he used disqualification in the sub headline and then followed it by two inclusion statements (If...Then). That's powerful!

Plant your flag: This is a very intimidating technique and shows no sign of neediness. Just imagine a guy that keeps pestering a hot chick at the bar. It's a massive turn off and she won't be attracted to his neediness at all. Same goes in business folks. For example: *"When the slots fill up and there's no seats left, your payment will be immediately returned, and you won't be able to buy tickets at the door".*

Tidal wave: You want to show the reader that loads of people are already buying. Not only does this inject some urgency into the close and gets them to act today, it also carries a form of social proof. If all these people are already buying, then the reader thinks it's "safe". For example: *"We have thousands of readers and 80% of them have already taken advantage of this limited offer. If our phone lines are busy, please be patient. We've hired a virtual customer support, so hopefully you can get through".*

Lagoon: This is just the opposite to the tidal wave. It's like an inclusion statement to speak directly to the reader, but framed in a way that it's not for everyone. It's mainly appealing when selling high-end products and exclusivity. For example: *"We've tried our best to get this in the hands of people that value luxury. Only one out of fifty people will respond to this".* This gets all the people that value exclusivity to purchase and excludes all others".

14. Two Choices (crossroads)

This gets the reader thinking about his future and really digs deep into his motivations and desires. Either way, you're closing him here, whether it's a no or yes. For example:
"You have two choices; you can do what you've always done and get the same old results. Or you could take advantage of the opportunity today and invest in the course that may change your life altogether. On average 95% of the population retire and have no investment savings for themselves and their kids. So, you can be one of the average people, and keep doing what you've always done, and get the same results. Or you could make a no risk, life-changing decision and take the leap today".

See, this really gets his blood boiling. No one wants to be like the "average person" and especially in that rough situation later in life. You're really tapping into deep desires to take action.

15. Personal mission

You may have heard people say something like, *"This is not about the money. I have enough of that, it's all about helping you achieve true freedom, not me"*. Now, this is somewhat true and also false. Because if you didn't care about the money, why wouldn't you give it away for free? On the other hand, if you did give it away for free, no one would value it. Anyway, the point of this "personal mission" is to position the offer like you're doing them a massive favor, rather than trying to hard "sell" them. Take this example:

> I've already made more than enough money to support my family using this strategy...
>
> And now I want to help ordinary folks who don't have access to the wealth-building strategies of the global elite.
>
> I never felt "right" rigging the machine to help the rich get richer.
>
> And after my kids were born (I've got seven!)... I saw what life was really about.
>
> Not just becoming rich and happy, but to pursue a *meaningful cause*...
>
> Something that would make my family proud.
>
> That's why I'm on a mission to make this opportunity available to everyday folks like you.
>
> My goal is to help 100 regular Americans set themselves up for a chance to become certified millionaires.

Do you see what I mean? He positioned himself at the top of the mountain and is offering the prospects a guide to get to the top with his help. He's already been there and done it. It's not about money now; it's about helping people (noble cause). When using this personal mission technique, make sure that you always provide a... **believable reason why**, just like the writer did here.

16. Price anchors

There are a few ways to use these, but here I will just cover the basics. The main purpose behind price anchors is getting the client accustomed to seeing and accepting the higher figures; and then, when you drop the price and deliver the sucker punch, the offer will appear even more irresistible. This makes use of the **compare and contrast** persuasion principle.

Even though the prospect may know about price anchors, it still works at a subconscious level. It's like dipping your feet in ice cold water and then hot water. The contrast will make the hot water feel like lava. If, however, you had your feet in lukewarm water, and then hot water, it wouldn't provide the same contrast. Same goes for price.

Here's a way to really use price anchors effectively. It's more applicable to presentations (webinars) than a sales letter. Get a pen and paper and follow me here. This is life changing!

You want to get the prospect to:

[1] Commit to the higher price before the call to action. If it's possible, try to do it early in the sales message after building desire and intrigue. To get them to accept the higher price and [2] make a commitment, you must [3] demonstrate that you're selling money at a discount.

STEP 1: Selling money at a discount

"Would you give me $50,000 for a sales letter, if I increased your revenue from $100,000 per month to $250,000?"

At this point [1] I've anchored the price of $50,000 and [2] got them to commit to a no-brainer proposition.

STEP 2: Get them to make a commitment

"Yes".

From here, you can build more desire for the product and then when it comes time for the close [3], you can drop the price as a fast action bonus.

STEP 3: Drop the price as a fast action bonus

"The total value of all of this is $50,000. Do you remember that number? Good! Because I know, without a shadow of a doubt, I will pull in more than $250,000 for your business. Now, obviously I'm not going to charge you $50,000, even though you committed to it earlier. Let's say I did charge you $50,000. Would it be worth it, if you could put $1 in and get $5 out? Of course, it would! When you sign up in the next 30 minutes, you can get it for only $25,000".

This formula here is very, very, very effective. You've got the prospect to accept the $50,000 --- (**pre-established anchored price**). After building so much desire and anticipation in the start and middle of the presentation, the prospect is already prepared to fork over $50,000. But, when you drop to the fast action bonus price ($25,000), they feel like they're getting a screaming deal. Here's an example of price anchors in a sales letter:

$27,000, $42,333 and even an extraordinary $95,833 in a Matter of DAYS

How much would that be worth to you?   Future pace

Before you answer, consider this... open loop

When I used to run a hedge fund...

We used to charge something called the 2-and-20 fee structure...

Meaning you are charged a 2% management fee...   Apples to Oranges

AND you give the fund 20% of your returns.   Comparison

Remember how I said the One-Day Bonus Indicator showed it could deliver average returns totaling $24,829 every 9 days?

That equates to $1,390,424 a year.

With gains like that...

Your fees would easily be over $250,000   PRICE ANCHOR

---

17. Price drops / justifications

It drives me through the wall when I see people make this same mistake. You'll see the rookie marketers advertise a discount like this: *"The business blueprint is now on sale for $297"*. Here's the thing: When you drop the price like this and provide no believable reason why, the prospect will know you're full of shit. He's heard that phrase a dozen times in the last hour. Not only does this hurt the first sale, it also hurts the residual sales on the back-end, because they won't believe you anymore. When you have a ***believable reason why***, it changes the game. It makes the prospect feel as though he really is getting a deal.

Look at these examples:

Can you see how the writer ties everything in? He didn't pull the $250,000 out of thin air; there was a reason for the price (4th sentence). See how the writer used a reframe (9 days to 1 year)?

Remember how I said the One-Day Bonus Indicator showed it could deliver average returns totaling $24,829 every 9 days?

That equates to *$1,390,424 a year...*

With gains like that...

Your fees would easily be over $250,000.

And to be fair...

With potential returns like that...

I think that's worth every penny...

But don't worry.

The special membership to **The Buyout Millionaire Club** won't cost anywhere near $250,000.

It won't even cost $50,000.

Not even $10,000...

Once he has established this, he starts dropping the price one more "level" with a **reason why**. Look how he went from $5,000 to $2,000 (next page). He showed the reader how it could potentially pay for itself, and most importantly, gave a **reason why** he dropped the price even further. To put icing on the cake, he also provided a reason for the $5,000 figure. The "publishing price".

$5,000 is an incredible deal.

And this membership could potentially pay for itself many times over by next week.

But I understand you're not familiar with the One-Day Bonus Indicator...

After all, it's inspired by a system only hedge funds have access to.

But because I want to be the first man at Agora Financial to help create 100 millionaires from regular Americans...

I am going to lower the cost of admission to $2,000.

That's a full $3,000 off the already incredible publishing price of $5,000.

18. Presuppose

*"**When** you sign up for The Domino Report, I'll give you a full year to test out the service at no risk to you"*.

You must assume the sale. The word "**When**" pre – supposes the action. I will cover this in more detail later. For now, let's cover the basics. Be very careful when using the word "If" when you're writing the closing / offer section. Unless you're making an inclusion statement (If...then), always use "when". It pre-supposes the prospect will buy the product and gets the reader to imagine having the product already (future pace).

19. Ownership

Show the prospect that the product is already in his possession and it's specifically for him. Look at the difference:

*"You'll get **your** specially-made replica suit"* (ownership)

*"You'll get **the** specially made "replica" suit"*.

20. Urgency and scarcity

Boy, oh boy, are these two persuasion triggers like dynamite! In most cases, these are used in the offer section of the sales letter, but it's also a good idea to sprinkle them in throughout. The main purpose of both is to set a fire underneath the prospect's butt and get him to take action. They both tap into the hardwiring of our human psychology.

Urgency: This is really all about telling your prospect that time is ticking and action needs to be taken. The longer they wait and sit around "thinking about it", they run the risk of missing out. Think of a deadline. This really gets you moving, especially when it comes to the last few days or even hours.

Unethical marketers will use fake countdown timers that reset after refreshing the page. Don't get me wrong, count down timers are really effective when used ethically and honestly. If you've ever been to a seminar and seen a platform sales person sell millions worth of products, you'll see at the end, they always use a countdown timer or set some sort of deadline.

Scarcity: The scarcer a product or service is, the more we desire it, and thereby increases the perceived value automatically. This is all about telling your prospect there's a limited quantity. And if they wait, they will pay the consequences of paying higher prices, waiting longer, or missing out entirely. A fast action bonus is a very popular way to create scarcity, or maybe "first come, first served" if they are the first five out of fifteen.

Scarcity always creates urgency, but not the other way around. Here's why: If there's a deadline, it will create urgency, because time is running out. That said, if there's no scarcity, they'll think "Okay, no worries. I can probably buy the product next time". Now, here's how scarcity leads to both:

Let's say you've got 800,000 readers on your list, but you've only printed 150 copies of your new book *because* of delivery issues. This really creates a lot more demand than there is supply. It leads to scarcity, but at the same time, also urgency (because if they don't act now, the other subscribers will get in before them). Here are some examples, in the same promotion.

> But as I mentioned, this playbook is NOT for sale.
>
> I'm only making it available for my readers.
>
> That means you can have it today for FREE...

> It's worth noting, you WON'T be able to find a copy of this playbook for sale on Amazon...
>
> In fact, you won't be able to find it for sale anywhere else online, at any price...
>
> But today, I'd like to give you a copy for FREE.

> And every month, I publish these incredible opportunities for over 88,350 readers through my investing research advisory called *Technology Profits Confidential*.

> This may be your only and last chance to turn $100 into a retirement fortune. And if you miss out, you'll spend the rest of your life regretting it. So while there's still time left, click below to get started.
>
> Remember, this is strictly limited to the first 250 people who respond today. If I don't hear from you soon, I'll be forced to add your name to a waiting list.

You have to show the prospect what they will **lose** if they don't act now. You must make them literally feel and see through their minds eye, what they're about to miss out on if they wait because of the deadline. **Always** provide a **reason why**, as I've said all throughout the book. You'll see marketers all the time say "1 hour left" or something along those lines. Prospects have heard this language so often; their bullshit detector is already going off. But, provide a reason like "the servers on the website are closing in one hour because of an overload of visitors and it's crashing the site. If it goes on any longer, the entire site will break. For that reason, you have 1 hour left".

Admittedly, that's a very bad example, but even so, it shows that as long as you provide a reason why... it makes everything more believable. The real magic really comes from the sentence that proceeds the "sucker punch". The first paragraph acts as the "set-up" to show the already existing demand.

Let me give you an example:

"And every month I share some of these secrets to my 112,343 readers through my newsletter called Killer Copy. Occasionally, I'll reveal some new secrets to the 1.2 million people following me on Facebook".

The next paragraph simply states the limited amount and reason why. Because of the paragraph before, the prospect knows over 1.2 million are going to see this same message. It injects serious amounts of urgency and scarcity.

"As you already know, I only have 250 copies available because of the market test I've arranged with my book publisher. That's why I suggest you claim your copy before they run out".

Here's another example of scarcity + reason why:

That's why we're proud to release **The "501(k)" Plan: How to Fully Fund Your Own Worry-Free Retirement—Starting at Any Age**, which gives a blueprint anyone can use to retire years faster... *without* Wall Street.

We have printed 5,000 copies of the book that we are giving out for free. We're doing this because we believe there's a vastly better way for Americans to retire today. And we want to prove it.

So, please, enjoy the book at our expense.

All we ask is you cover the small cost of shipping the book to your door.

Already, hundreds of free copies have been claimed.

And if you want to claim one of the few remaining FREE copies, we suggest you act fast...

Just click on the link below to secure your free copy while they are still available.

When selling information products like an e-newsletter, you can't really play on scarcity by saying "300" newsletters left. That's pure lies. Here's the solution: You play on the fact that the prospect might miss out on the **opportunity** [marijuana stocks] in this example.

> Because if you wait until after that happens, these marijuana stocks will no longer be trading for pennies...
>
> And your chance to amass a retirement fortune starting with a single $100 bill will disappear forever.

21. Explain how to use the product

This can be very easily overlooked, and it's a really important point to address, especially when selling certain products. If you were selling a consumable product like a nutritional drink, make sure you tell the prospect how many servings per shake, how many shakes to have a day and so on. Make everything very simple and easy to understand.

22. Before you're done, summarize

After writing a killer sales letter, one of the worst things you can do is miss the summary of the offer. You'll have different types of readers. Some will read every word; some will scan the sub-heads and some will go straight to the call to action. Here's an example:

> P.S. As I've shown you today, many of these marijuana companies have EXPLODED **8,500%**, **11,430%**, **17,054%**, **25,099%** and even **127,900%**. And that's why you need this *Marijuana Millionaire Playbook*... to discover how to take part in what historians will call the biggest boom EVER.
>
> This may be your only and last chance to turn $100 into a retirement fortune. And if you miss out, you'll spend the rest of your life regretting it. So while there's still time left, click below to get started.

23. The re-cap

Just before you give a call to action you might want to do a re-cap: There are two primary ways to do this. Let's go back to the fishing example. You can either take the:

1. **Wide net approach** and attempt to catch as many (sardines) as possible. This is where you appeal to a broad range of benefits and appeals. Instead of hammering down on one desire, you take a step back and show the prospect how it will help in other areas of life. Let's use the example of a copywriting course:

"Think of the advantage in **business**; you never have to make another cold call again. Think of the impression you'll make when you know how to communicate with the **opposite sex**. Think of the complete freedom you'll have to **travel** anywhere in the entire world... You'll be able to experience **different cultures**... You'll be able to spend time with your **loved ones** and be **recognized** at every high-level mastermind".

2. **One line, one hook approach** where you focus on just one main desire. Instead of tossing a net into the ocean, you're now focused on catching one fish only – the Marlin.

"It frees you forever from **cold calls** and wasting time on unqualified prospects... It frees you forever from having **100 telemarketing employees**... It frees you forever from **long, hard hours of face-to-face sales**... It means that when you master this, you can leverage your time and **have prospects coming to you,** even while you sleep... It means that you can **scale your business controllably**... It means that you can provide a **shot of revenue almost on demand"**. In a nutshell, the second approach provides all the benefits in one area (business) where the first approach has a wider appeal (all areas of life).

GUARANTEE

Whenever a transaction occurs between two people, one must take more risk than the other. And by the way, every situation you find yourself in has risk associated with it. After building desire for the product and getting the prospect to salivate, you need to do one more thing: Take that damn boulder out of his backpack so he has less load on his shoulders.

Make it as easy as possible for him. Give him all the reasons to respond. Remember, he doesn't want to look stupid in front of other people. Give him all the excuses and reassurances he needs. Reversing the risk for the prospect is huge. There must be little to no risk; just to push him over the edge. Generally, the longer the guarantee, the more likely the prospect will forget about it. Usually, they will make the decision for a refund in the first fourteen days or so. Anything after this, and they forget (in most cases). Here are some variations of the guarantee:

- Basic money back guarantee.
- Refund and keep all the bonuses.
- Repetition of guarantee throughout the sales message.
- Free trial offer.
- Primary focus of the sales message (lead with it in the headline).

Tip him over with a guarantee. Look at this performance guarantee for bicycle tires and how it takes away all the risk.

"First, test them for a full month for lighting speed... During that very first month alone:

1. These tires must give you up to 50 RPMs instantly, or your full purchase back!

2. These tires must save you up to five minutes from your regular journey instantly, or your full purchase back!

3. As an extra added assurance: these tires must continue to give you this speed, performance, and time savings for two full years, or I'll will send you a brand-new set absolutely free!".

CLEAR CALL TO ACTION (CTA)

Give one very clear call to action. Tell 'em what happens after you click the button, tell them exactly what to do and what to expect once they've taken the action. Here's an example,

> That's my personal guarantee.
>
> To get started... simply click the button that you see below..
>
> Hitting this button does not obligate you to anything.
>
> You'll just be directed to another page, where you can review all of the details of this special offer.

After telling the prospect the product is $2,000, the writer must re-assure the reader that the payment won't come out just by clicking the button. Even though this sounds obvious for a lot of people, it's not so obvious for others. The target prospect is an elderly person, and generally speaking, they have more skepticism to making payments online. Take away as much risk as possible and tap into the hardwired emotion. security.

HOW TO MAKE YOUR $144,000 PRODUCT SEEM AS INEXPENSIVE AS A CUP OF COFFEE

To make your expensive products appear inexpensive and jump off the shelves, follow this recipe. Here are the 3 criteria:

1. Making it irrelevant

A lot of people always wonder how I charge such a premium for a sales letter. First, they don't understand that copy is king. Copywriting is not an expense in a business. It could well be one of the best investments a business owner can make. Would you give me $10,000 if you got $50,000 back in the next few weeks? Or would you give me $50,000 if you got $250,000 in the next few months? Of course, you would! That's how lucrative this skill is. The "price" is irrelevant. Let's take a hypothetical example:

A client just paid **$10,000** for a sales letter. It converts at **10%** at a price point of **$49**. You're sending **1,000** people to the online sales page every day. That is $4,900 every day [100 x 49]. That's an average of $147,000 per month. Let's say the advertising cost is 50% and we're selling info products, which means no fulfilment cost. The **net profit is $73,500** in the first month alone. Never mind all the other back-end sales and all the other months or years this promotion will be running.

So, you put $10,000 in and got $73,500 out—in one month. Not a bad return. Even if the "conversion rate" was 5%, it would still give you $36,750.

Here's another example: Let's say I accepted you as a client and we were a good fit for each other. The task is to write a sales letter and our agreement was royalties only on the percentage increase from the current control.

Let's say you had a conversion rate of **3%** on the front-end. I came in and got it to **5%**. All you must do as a business owner to make this pay for itself is... raise the shipping and handling fee and you're good to go. No out of pocket money for you.

2. Rationale

I've been talking a lot about giving a reason why throughout this book and there's a very good reason for it. See what I did there? Always give a reason why! You see, there's tremendous power when you use the word "because". Once you give a reason behind the action, the resistance fades away. Take this example (Copywriting Training Course):

"The investment for this video course is $2,000"
"The investment for this video course is $2,000 **because** *the seminar attendees got the exact same secrets, and had to pay $4,000 for the seminar, as well as $1,000 for travel expenses. All together it costs each person on average $5,000".*

What a difference! After reading the second one, can you see why the price is $2,000 and how you're getting a much better deal than previous students? Before you write your sales letter, it's a good idea to make a no-brainer offer. And when doing this, look for ways you can use the power of rationale to show the prospect why the "value" is what it is.

3. The proposition is accepted as reasonable

Do you remember what we spoke about earlier when talking about price anchoring? I mentioned "Pre-established value". This is where you set up a pre-existing condition. For example, let's say you paid me $24,000 for a full-day consulting session. That's now a pre-existing condition. Essentially, this is what's happening: You've accepted that $24,000 is worth one day of my time. From here, the only thing left to do when selling you the next product, is make it sound reasonable. Here's how:

"Okay, great! It seems like I can help you. I'd need to write a Facebook Ad, Landing Page, Sales Page, and One Upsell. That would take me three days. Would you agree with this?

Once I've done that, I'd need to write all the follow up emails and script the re-targeting videos. That should take me one day. Sound fair?

Lastly, I will need to write the down-sell script and some more follow up emails. This should take about an extra two days. Does this sound reasonable?"

It's very unlikely the prospect won't agree with you, as you go through the process step-by-step. Once you've got them to agree and believe six days is fair and reasonable, then you're off to the races.

Because the $24,000 number is already reasonable and accepted (already paid $24,000 for one day). From here, you take that same number and just multiply it by the amount of days it will take [$24,000 x 6=$144,000]. That seems more reasonable.

Just imagine if someone asked, *"How much do you charge for a full marketing campaign?"* and you say "$144,000". That sounds like an astronomical number just for a few words on paper. But... give the logical reason behind this, and prospects will be more willing to accept it.

MAKE YOUR PRODUCT SEEM LIKE A STEAL

Use value building words / phrases: There are many ways to communicate this without using the same words per se. These words just by themselves increase the perceived value of the product. Read this:

"You'll pay *only* a *tiny fraction* of that...*just* $49!"

Now, read this:

"The investment for the newsletter is $49".

Wowie! That's a hard stop. Without the words "only", "tiny", "fraction" and "just", the price is a lot more intimidating. Once you start looking for these "value building words" you'll see them pop up everywhere.

Price comparison + reframe: I mentioned reframing earlier on, but I think it's worth repeating and showing how impactful it is when working with price. Pay attention to the reframe and price comparison. All these techniques give the prospect more perspective and reference points for comparison. Here's the example:

"Up to this point, the newsletter sold for as high as $49 per month. But I thought $588 is more than most people are willing to invest, so that's why I've arranged to get the price so low, that this newsletter would pay for itself twelve times over in one year when using these investment strategies... If you act now, it's only $24.50 per month".

Did you catch it?

1. I gave the higher price (per **month** - $49) and (1 **year** - $588).
2. I showed the prospect how it will pay for itself in one year alone.
3. Finally, the sucker punch... I dropped the price and went back to the monthly price of $24.50.

Pretty cool, huh?

Value + reward: Here you show the prospect how he will benefit from the product and at the same time how it will pay for itself.

If we go back to our example:

1. You'll see the prospect gets the **benefit**— *"using these investment strategies..."*
2. **Pay for itself** - *"would pay for itself..."*
3. The money saved is compared to a **higher figure** - *"12 times over in one year"*.

Introduce a condition + positioning:

"If you will check your sales before and after implementing the copywriting techniques, then tell your friends and family about the results, here is what I am prepared to do for you...".

1. I introduced an action you must take *("If...then" statement)*

2. Plus, I framed it in a way that I'm doing you a favor, not the other way around (*"here is what I am prepared to do for you"*)

3. More words to give the feeling of favor: *"Prepared to do"*, *"I'll give you"*, *"You can have"*.

THE 7 GOLDEN PERSUASION SECRETS

What I'm about to share with you, comes from the work of Blair Warren. These persuasion triggers are used all throughout copy.

People have to convince themselves and come to their own conclusions. Instead of telling them you're a multimillionaire, **show** them through demonstration (pictures and actions). Picture this: A guy wearing a Tom Ford 3-piece navy suit. He pulls up in a Rolls Royce. His bodyguard escorts him on his way to the conference room in the hotel while his driver waits outside until he is finished. I didn't have to tell you this guy has some money. You came to that conclusion yourself. The point: There are already symbols that represent certain things and people come to their own conclusions. When you write copy, think about the pictures you use, and what they demonstrate.

Persuasion Trigger #1: People need to feel needed.

People are drawn to people who need them. Who doesn't need a sense that their life matters? You can communicate this by simply saying, "I need your help here, because I can give you all the information in the world about copywriting but…".

Persuasion Trigger #2: People will do anything to gain a sense of hope.

Focus on the **meaning** of the product, not so much the benefits. Think of the promise that you can make to persuade others and provide hope. Talking about hope… do you remember the importance of the Unique Mechanism? It too gives HOPE!

Look at the picture below. The writer uses a testimonial story to show the reader that loads of other people have done it before, and there's no reason why he can't. This gives him hope! One of the biggest reasons people don't buy, is due to limiting internal beliefs.

> And you could do the same as him...
>
> After all, he's just one of literally hundreds of folks whose lives have been changed forever.

One of the best ways to overcome this, is by using the **chain of belief**. Start with the facts that he already accepts and believes. Now show him through logical steps how it's possible to achieve his desired end result. You must make it so logical that it becomes undeniable. Even though there are many ways to give the prospect a sense of hope, almost nothing is as important as showing the reader the results of previous customers that have gone through the same process. The reader must **identify** with them.

> This is the true "get rich quick" opportunity you've spent your whole life waiting for...

Persuasion Trigger #3: People need a scapegoat / enemy to blame.

Example: *"If you've gone on the Keto diet and re-gained all the weight, it's not your fault. It's Keto"*. Agora Financial always use Wall Street as the scapegoat:

> **YOU can claim your own "One-Day Bonus" from these massive buyouts... Without working a SINGLE day on Wall Street.** ENEMY

People generally seek someone else to blame for their circumstances and deep inside, feel that others have been withholding something from them. The avatar from Agora Financial believe that Wall Street insiders know all the secrets, but they don't want to reveal them to the public.

And do you know the best part of all this? The person that identifies and labels the problem, becomes the "hero". For example:

"The real reason why you haven't heard about this tax loophole is because Wall Street Insiders had to sign a disclosure agreement in 1994 to keep the information inside the walls. They have refused to reveal this information to people like you, and once you know how to do this, you'll be saving as much as $500 per month".

When using the scapegoat, you're also creating an **Us vs Them** feeling. The quickest way to be ignored is to say the same thing everyone else is saying. You want to be polarizing, and this is exactly the way to do it. You may have heard the term "throw rocks at the enemies". This is exactly what it is.

You may be wondering, "If I use a competitor or enemy as a scapegoat, I might lose a lot of potential buyers...". Hang on here, I got you! When using this strategy, you talk directly to your target prospect. All the other people will quit reading immediately anyway. But that's fine, because if you've written your headline properly, you've attracted and flagged down your target prospect. Forget 95% of the people in the market. You want to get in the head of and speak directly to the 5% that will buy. Although it may seem like you're taking a massive risk by standing for something, it's the complete opposite. You create a stronger bond with the target audience.

The **Us vs Them** method is used frequently—and for good reason. It works because it shows the reader that you and him share the same values. It also adds more believability throughout the rest of the copy. You'll often see words like "our" and "we" used to "group" and bond with the reader.

	NEW Opportunity	Action word	Offering HOPE! + "OUR" lifetime = Us vs Them
We will NEVER see an opportunity even remotely like this again in our lifetime.			

Donald Trump is a persuasion expert; make no mistake. His messaging is always very polarizing—it attracts his target audience, and creates a tight bond, while at the same time generating publicity from the "haters" he doesn't want to attract anyway. Very smart move!

Persuasion Trigger #4: People need to be noticed and feel understood.

You need to show empathy. They key word: **show**. It's great to say "Listen, I understand..." It's even better to tell a story that demonstrates that you really understand. The story must identify with the reader, regardless of the form. It could be a third-person testimonial story or your own story. A way to create this feeling of empathy is by echoing the prospect's thoughts back to them. And where do these thoughts come from? Simple. The prospect's mental model of the world. You cannot understand their model of the world without in-depth market research. Let's take the Agora Financial reader:

"You may feel like Wall Street is keep their cards close to their chest". Damn, that's really going to connect with them. They already think this! Remember, everyone is telling themselves a story. If you can meet the prospect where he is at (his ongoing internal story) and feed it back to him, you've unlocked the persuasion vault.

As humans, when we find out that another person thinks, believes, and feels just like we do, we feel validated and understood. That's why knowing the reader and using their language is very important. The difference between great and poor copywriters is—drum roll please—market research.

Persuasion Trigger #5: People need to know things others don't know.

Why do you think the word "secrets" is used so often? Not because it's a great-looking word. It's because it taps into our deep primal hardwiring. For some reason, we as humans are always looking for the magic bullet or secret. We always gravitate to the path of least resistance. You may be doing it in some areas of your life, perhaps in fitness or maybe even business. Secrets convey mystery and knowing things other people don't know. As mentioned earlier, this makes the product seem all the more valuable. I refer to this persuasion trigger as "being in the know" or "insider knowledge". When you share secrets and new information with your prospects and give them an "aha" moment, a sense of bonding occurs.

Here's an example:

Again, it's all about communicating with the deeper structure. You can use many words or phrases to communicate the same thing.

Persuasion Trigger #6: People need to be right.

You'll often see the words "It's not your fault". Never tell someone they're wrong and it's their fault. You'll never persuade them like that. Blame the vehicle or tool, not the person. Don't shoot the messenger! For example:

"If you're kicking yourself for missing these huge buyouts in the past... don't 'worry... it's not your fault".

Persuasion Trigger #7: People need to feel a sense of power.

Give a person a sense of choice. Whenever you push someone to do something, it creates resistance. The more you push, the more resistance is created. By giving the prospect a sense of choice, you create little resistance. There's a very effective way to bypass resistance and yet, still get the prospect to take the action you'd like them to take. I'm going to reveal that later. Think back to a time when someone told you what to do and gave you no choice. Maybe it was that time when your mother said, "You must eat the vegetables before candy!" Boy, oh boy, does that cause resistance!

Here's an example that gives the reader a "choice":

"But it's up to you to make those things a reality. Whether you choose to take us up on our offer today or sleep on it. It's your call".

The Nostradamus Secret

People predict future events all the time, and when you do this right, it's a killer for persuasion. The main reason this works so well, is because you're pre-framing the future event... and when the result you have predicted does occur, it's framed as an element of **positive proof**. Take this as an example:

Let's say I got you doing the Ketogenic diet today and gave you an entire explanation of why it's so effective and the best thing since sliced bread. Just before I finish the conversation, I tell you what you will see in the next two days. That is: your weight will drop drastically, if you follow the procedure I laid out for you. If you know anything about the Keto diet, it's basically low carb. The more carbs you eat, the more water you tend to hold. Well, knowing this, doesn't it make sense the weight will drop in a few days? Yes, it does! Because I know this ahead of time, I can predict and present the future result as positive **proof** that this diet really works! When predicting the future, just make sure you're certain that the future result will occur, otherwise belief will sink down the drain.

Context is king. We give people much power just based on a label.

Just recently, I went to the hospital to get my foot checked out because I stepped on a nail. I waited around for about ten minutes and when the nurse saw me, she told me that I would need to get an injection. I accepted her message, mainly because of the context I found myself in; the first element was the environment—the hospital. The fact that she was a "nurse" meant I automatically accepted her statement without question. Fast forward another two hours and thirty minutes, and I see the specialist. I planted my ass on the plastic chair, and in two minutes, she told me that I didn't need an injection.

The point: Context is king, and content comes second. The nurse probably could've told me to jump up and down, touch my toes, and I probably still would've done it. I automatically trusted the "specialist", took her word for it and left. Context is powerful.

Here's another example:

152

There are some cringey internet marketers on the internet that take pictures next to cars and private jets and then slowly leak them out as if it's theirs. It's context. They're demonstrating financial success and letting the reader come to their own conclusions. Nothing stops them from shooting a few videos in a fancy location and renting a Lamborghini. The point is that certain objects have built in labels and once we assign it to someone, they automatically become a "guru".

5 PERSUASION SECRETS TO MAKE YOURSELF LARGER THAN LIFE

1. Find patterns and show them

One of the best ways to establish massive credibility and respect from the reader is to demonstrate the "pattern" and why it works. Simplifying complex issues gives you superpowers. Many people use "formulas" to make this happen.

It's the founder of the pattern that gets the most power. An example in direct response marketing is Jay Abraham's *Only 3 Ways to Grow a Business*. It is referenced regularly and it always goes back to Jay. As far as I know, he was the "founder" of this concept, or at the very least he made it known to the public.

This is key: as long as you're the first one to make it known to the public, in their eyes you're seen as the founder. All power goes back to Jay for his discovery. Just like Jay Abraham, once you can identify a new pattern and point it out to people, you will also be continuously referenced by others and therefore create an army of credibility builders.

2. Your knowledge comes from a mysterious source

Remember, all throughout the sales message you need to show the prospect the **only** way he can get this product, is through the sales page and the personality or guru. You must show them you have knowledge that is not available to the "average" person on the street. You do this by using mysterious sources like:

- Very complex looking images (implies the reader can only figure this out with the help of the personality).
- A great story: "*I used to work in Wall Street and learned all the secrets behind closed doors that were kept from the*

public. And today, I wanted to share them with you as my personal mission is to create more self-made millionaires".

- Qualifications.
- Unique experience that almost no one has ever had.
- Any other established credible source.

It comes back to "being in the know" and showing that it's **new**! Remember, if the prospect has heard it before, he's out like a shot!

3. Be a label maker

Label the experiences and events that have happened to your prospects and customers. This will create a sense of security and understanding like no other. That's exactly why you should be showing the prospect from beginning to end that the product is "**safe**". Labels do this by providing a sense of simplicity and ease.

Here's a quality example: In the 1800s and early 1900s "Big Ideas" were called "concepts". It's the same thing, but different label. I think it was David Ogilvy that popularized the "Big Idea". This gave him massive credibility, although he didn't actually invent the concept.

Claude Hopkins talked about "schemes". Nowadays, "schemes" are called "offers". Creating new labels is basically a form of **neologizing** (a fancy word for coining something new) and acts as a form of proof which increases believability.

Here's how it's used in copywriting: Oftentimes, the "guru" will say something like this:

*"Once you know how these "**X-Markers**" work, you'll see returns like you've never seen before, and the best part... there's no risk, when you know what you're doing".*—He created a new label (X—Markers).

4. Give them a sense of power

This emotion is like playing with fire. Power can make people behave in strange ways. Just look at all the "leaders" as an example. Hitler thrived on power. Trump thrives on power. Managers thrive on power. Your job is to give your prospect the power to make a buying decision and take action. Keep in mind, people don't like being changed. They resist and resent it. That said, people are still willing and able to change. They must just **feel** like they have a sense of power and it's their decision. This interlinks with the "two choices close"— you must give them a choice.

Here's a **"formula"** that you can use (see what I did there?):

[1] Empathize with past failures and current problems.
[2] Ask permission.
[3] Tell them it's their decision.

Example: "You've read the letter to this point, which means you're rather interested in this opportunity. [1] I **get it**, you've probably **tried many "get rich quick" courses and you've seen no results**. And it's not your fault. You see, they didn't teach you the number one most important skill to develop for long term wealth. Now,[2] **with your permission**, I'd like to invite you to take advantage of this offer. I've done everything I can from here on, [3] **it's your decision to change your destiny**".

5. Make yourself difficult to reach

This of course, applies to anything the prospect does **before** the sales message. Not only do you derive humongous price desensitization benefits, you also attract better customers. Both Dan Kennedy and I apply this principle religiously. Dan is a champion at this. He's mastered this to a "T". He once said, "there is no long line to get to the wise man at the bottom of the mountain". He doesn't have a contact number that you can call him on—not even an email address. You basically can't contact him without jumping through many, many hoops. I believe you have to speak to his assistant, send a fax, and then she looks at it and decides if it should go into Dan's pile. The pile is attended to after a few weeks or months. If Dan does get to your message, he will fax it back.

The process is very long and tedious, just to make one communication with him. (The process isn't exactly like this, but it's near enough).

Here's another example from Dan:

Whenever his consulting clients want to pay him $18,600 for one day consulting, they must stay at a specific hotel (which, if I remember correctly, is not the most luxurious in the world). The process is drawn out, believe me. At this point, the poor person has probably travelled thousands of miles, through busy airports and has been dealing with busy crowds—altogether not a very pleasant experience for most people. I wouldn't be surprised if Dan picked them up in a rusty Jeep Renegade either. (Again, this isn't 100% accurate, however it illustrates the power Dan will get from these people jumping through so many hoops.

All this diminishes price resistance to rock bottom. He is making the client qualify himself so at the end they will literally be begging to work with Dan. This is a classic example of positioning.

You now have most, if not all, the copywriting knowledge you'll ever need. Throughout the book, I have been talking about *The Forbidden Secret*. Now, it's time to sink your teeth into the **chains of belief** and their deeper structures.

But just before we do, are you seeing the lesson within the lesson? Instead of reading the book as is... pay attention to how I'm applying the same techniques I'm teaching you.

If you haven't been doing that until now... don't worry, because what you're about to witness is a game changer!

HYPNOTIC TECHNIQUES IN COPYWRITING

A s we've already established, without belief, no one buys. Knowing this, you can begin to identify your prospect's beliefs by listening (through market research).

When I say "listening", it could be through forums, reviews, and groups. It doesn't necessarily have to be in a face-to-face or telephone conversation. Here are the structures of belief statements:

1. X **causes** Y **(cause and effect)**
2. X **means** Y **(complex equivalent)**

1. Cause and effect

The unconscious mind is always looking for **causality**. There are certain connective words or phrases that will scream **cause and effect**. The main idea of cause and effect is to link one idea to another. This is a natural form of communication and provides justification (logic) to the commitment. Here are some connective words:

"And, still, as, while, but, yet, **because**, before, after, while, whenever, so that, in the, if, although, same way that, therefore".

Pacing and Leading

Pacing: Where you match the reader's current experience and state what is true. Example: *"As you read these words, you're breathing in and out"*. These are true and undeniable statements.

Remember, stay away from the word "If". Always use "when". You want to **pre - suppose** (assume) that the action is going to be taken "*when you sign up*".

Leading: Take the reader to a new place

The trick to use cause and effect effectively, is using a few pacing statements followed by a leading statement. To do this, you must have in-depth market research and know what experiences your prospects have had. Here's an example:
"*You've been reading these words about The Forbidden Secret of Copywriting* **and** finally begin to realize that copywriting is the number one skill for more financial freedom". The first part (italics) matches the reader's current experience (you've been reading this book)—you agree with that (pacing).

The second part takes the reader somewhere **new** with a (leading) statement. The first statement acts like a bridge to the new suggestion. You know how I've been talking about **inserting chain links one by one to create and maintain belief**? Well, this is the same principle, but applied in a smaller and different context.

Let's look at the differences that connective words have:

➢ **"Because"** gives more reason to believe.

"You'll love this book".

"You'll love this book **because** it gives you the quickest and easiest ways to use forbidden techniques to persuade your prospect".

➢ **"The more, the more"** sets up a causality.

"Watch these videos, you'll make more money.

"**The more** you watch these videos **the more money** you'll make".

➢ When you tie two sentences together with the word "**and**", it has a subtle way of implying that the first thing caused the second thing.

"This book gives you tons of information to grow your business; it has made millions".

"This book gives you tons of information to grow your business **and** it has made millions".

See the difference? The second sentence had two separate ideas; and merges them into one (the unconscious mind cannot stand there not being a relationship between the two sentences when the word "**and**" is included). They're convincing themselves—it's "their" idea.

Take this example; read it carefully:

*"These gold stocks that are trading for pennies will soon begin trading for $30... $50...$65... or maybe even $100 or more. **And** once they get expensive like that, it will be too late for you to get rich quick!".*

Read it again (without the word "And")

"These gold stocks that are trading for pennies will soon begin trading for $30... $50...$65... or maybe even $100 or more. Once they get expensive like that, it will be too late for you to get rich quick!".

Can you see the impact of this one word? Without "And" the claim seems a lot less believable and exaggerated. It almost seems rude.

2. Complex equivalence

The unconscious mind is also looking for **meaning**. An easy way to implement complex equivalence is by using the word "means". Complex equivalence is where one event is seen as synonymous. "X means Y".

Example: *"Having no money **means** you're unsuccessful"*.

Here's how it's used in copy:

> At $49 we risk losing money. To turn a profit, we need your repeat business.
>
> That means giving you a superior newsletter... one you're so thrilled with, you'll stay with us year after year.

HOW LANGUAGE FRAMES EXPERIENCE

You can use the same words, but a different connective and it will have a completely different meaning. It will direct your attention to certain aspects of an experience.

Check this example of the connective words: "But", "And", "Even though". For example, if your "typical" 9-5 worker says:

"It's Sunday today (**BUT**) tomorrow is Monday" > This shifts the attention on the concern (Monday) and neglects the fact that it's Sunday.

"It's Sunday today (**AND**) tomorrow is Monday > The events are equally emphasized.

"It's Sunday today (**EVEN THOUGH**) tomorrow is Monday > This focuses your attention more on the first statement (the fact that it's Sunday).

You've already seen an example of the word "and". Let me show you an example of "but". I like to call it the "pivot word".

> You'll spend the rest of your life regretting it.
>
> But luckily, amassing a fortune with these tiny marijuana stocks isn't hard.

See how the writer hammered on fear and then used "**but**" to pivot to the solution (product). He basically negated everything that came before the word "but". If you're a guy reading this, you know how this word can deliver a blow.

After dating a lovely lady, she says, "I had a great time and really enjoyed talking to you, but…" Anything that comes after this, doesn't matter.

Here's an example of the "If…Then" Inclusion statement:

"You could earn up to $5,000 per week, if you can write for three hours every day". Benefit and hard work have been linked together.

In the **foreground,** the major benefit has been brought up— "earn $5,000 per week"—makes the statement more motivating.

Now read this…

"If you can write for three hours every day, you could earn up to $5,000 a week". Same words, however the impact is diminished because the **foreground** has now changed to working hard.

Embedded commands

Earlier, I spoke about resistance and told you there's a way to get someone to do something without prompting resistance. Here it is. Embedded commands are where you put a statement inside a larger sentence. You use permissive language and frame it by asking a question. Look at the difference—which one prompts more resistance?

"Stop going on social media".

"I was *wondering* how many of you thought that it would be a good idea to **stop going on social media?**".

See how I communicated the same thing, but framed it differently? (embedded command in bold). The most important part of the sales message is gaining and keeping attention. You could have the best copy in the world, but if no one reads it what's the point? You need to get ATTENTION and maintain it. Here's how:

1. Asking a question (the obvious way).

2. Appeal to the reader's mental movie.

I mentioned the importance of painting pictures in the readers mind earlier. This is because **the customer is making his buying decision based upon a series of sensory constructs.** In other words, the prospect is sitting his ass down in the cinema; you're the narrator, and you're planning every single scene the prospect is about to witness in his mind's eye.

When it comes to the senses, only the **V**isual, **A**uditory and **K**inesthetic play a massive role in our daily lives. Now that we know the prospect is making a buying decision based on this sequence, how do we catch the most buyers and create a block- buster Oscar-award winning movie? Here's the formula:

1. Visual (SEE)
2. Auditory (HEAR)
3. Kinesthetic (FEEL)

Let's take this example: "After eating so many carbs, my stomach was literally like a **balloon**. It was about to **pop**. And even worse, I was moving like a **slug**. Even though yesterday at McDonalds, people were saying *I'm fat*, I kept eating. And to be honest, *deep beneath the surface*, I was shockingly *embarrassed* about it".

"Balloon" - Paints the picture in the readers mind.
"Pop" - Appeals to the auditory.
"Brutally embarrassed" - Appeals to the kinesthetic.

Look at the embedded suggestion *"I'm fat"*. Even though the sentence doesn't out right say the reader is fat, the unconscious mind of the reader hears "I'm fat".

This is a very powerful technique of persuasion, especially when you know your market very well. You're pushing the emotional buttons of the reader and agitating the conversation that's going on in their mind.

"Deep beneath the surface" acts as an embedded command to further get into a state of trance.

Use the language that the target reader is using. Again, you'll get all of this in the market research. If the word "shockingly embarrassed" keeps popping up, make sure to use it in your copy.

In essence, the writer is **"mind reading"**, but in reality, he knows what the prospect has experienced before (embarrassment every time they're seen eating by other people). Buyers make buying decisions based on their feelings—not their logical mind. So, the feeling state (kinesthetic) acts as the punch line.

Some things to consider when doing upsells: If you know anything about marketing funnels, you know that upsells are the lifeblood of a successful funnel. Would you like to know the six-word upsell that is responsible for trillions of dollars? Sure, you would! Here it is:

"Do you *want fries with that?"*

Why has this little phrase generated so much revenue? Well, let's think about the embedded command here. The command is framed as a **question**, but still commands the customers to purchase the fries *"you want fries with that"*.

Universal quantifier

The formula: Every time + problem

*"**Every time** I go to the local grocery haul, I can just see the clerks gossiping and calling me overweight. Admittedly, I do feel a sense of embarrassment **every time** I purchase another six doughnuts"*.

The word "every time" really intensifies the situation and suggests it's not going to get better in the present, nor the future. It intensifies the pain of the reader and then pushes them into a new direction.

It slips past the conscious mind and hammers the reader's deepest fear: never losing weight. The reason why this works, is because it's a hypnotic reminder.

Essentially, you're communicating with the "unspoken words". You need to know what the reader experiences daily— cough, cough—market research. Every overweight person is thinking the slim person is looking at them funny and saying, "You're overweight".

Did you catch the three sensory inputs being used? Visual *"see"*, Auditory *"gossiping"* and Kinesthetic *"embarrassed"?*

Universal quantifier pattern

These are all examples of negative future pacing. You're showing the reader the problem will continue to occur if they don't take action now.

*"**Every time you** look in the mirror you see a fat seal, **every time** you look in the mirror you're disgusted, **every time you** look in the mirror you know your friends and family are ashamed of you. But what if, **every time you** look in the mirror you see a Greek God exploding with confidence. Once you realize the power of this diet plan, you'll never have to worry about your physical appearance again."*

The repetitive nature of the universal quantifier "every time" adds impact when you state the benefit.

Trial closes

The more we say "yes" to someone, the easier it gets to say "yes" to them again. Here are some words to use:

"isn't it? is it not? aren't you? wasn't it? wouldn't you agree? haven't you? don't you? right?"

If you've been paying close attention, you'll see I've been using these trial closes all throughout. Listen: I like to exceed expectations. Here's a few more examples in action.

- "...second time is a charm, right?"...

- "Pretty amazing...right?"

- "Pretty terrifying position to be in...right?"

- "You're here because you want to scale your business...right?"

- "Each entrepreneur's company is different, right?"

- "...pretty cool, right?"

- "Would you give me $25,000 if I can get you 5 million bucks?"

- "Is that worth 25,000 bucks?"

- "...are you ok with that?"

- "You probably understand what copywriting is...right?"

- "Doesn't that sound a lot more efficient than door knocking?"

- "Now, to write copy, it doesn't look that complicated, right?"

- "Are you getting the power of this?"

- "Yep...pretty awesome, right?"

- "Pretty cool...right? "

- "Are you getting this?"

Commitment and consistency are two of my favorite persuasion triggers. Think about tribe members. Once they've done all the initiations, it's very difficult for them to return to their "normal" life, because they've formed a new identity. That's the power of small commitments. Just be a little careful with trial closes in sales letters. You don't want to use too many. Depending on the length of the sales letter, 2-4 is a good guideline. In a presentation like a webinar or platform speech, you can make use of these a lot more frequently.

> Likely never, right?
>
> You're not alone... nobody has EVER seen gains even REMOTELY close to this...

Mind reading

This is where you seem to know what the reader is thinking and feeling without a direct communication. The "secret" is to sound specific, even though you're making a vague statement.

For example:

*"You may be **thinking** this is another get rich quick course. And listen, **I know** you're **frustrated** because all these courses you've bought have given you zero skills, besides pulling out your wallet. **I know** what's best for you, because once you learn this invaluable financial skill, you'll never go without money".*

That is very scrappy copy, but I want you to focus on the principle. Did you see how I said, *"I know you're frustrated"*. That's a cold read and it can be done very effectively if you've done your —Wait for it —Market Research.

When you use this in copywriting, you are not just matching their experience; you're establishing credibility with your customer. To "mind read" effectively, insert "I wonder" before the question. It's a lot softer and prompts a little less resistance in the statement. There are also other softeners such as "probably", "maybe" and "likely". For example —pay close attention here to the resistance both statements provoke—

"Are you sick and tired of business courses that don't work?"

"**I wonder** if you're sick and tired of business courses that don't work?"

Ah, ah —see the difference? The second one also seems like you know what they're thinking without direct communication.

Nested loops

Open loops are used throughout copy to maintain attention and get the reader to read all the way through. The main purpose behind open loops is to open a curiosity gap, transition back to the body copy, and leave the reader wanting more. If you've ever watched a TV series, you know that at the end of every episode, they leave you on a cliff-hanger wanting more and making you want to find out what's happening next. That's what we're doing in our copy. Our minds cannot stand it when someone opens a loop and doesn't close it. The trick to creating open loops is to insert them after you've written the first draft. Because now you know what you've already written and can tease it beforehand. Like this:

Section A: The writer has teased and built intrigue for the product and now transitions to the credibility section.

Before I Show You How to Claim Your *Marijuana Millionaire Playbook*, Let Me Introduce Myself

---

Section B: After covering objections and providing the benefits, he inserts another open loop.

But today, I want you to have it for FREE.

I'll show you how to claim it in just a moment.

169

Section C— Offer section: He's built enough desire now and is heading into the close. Before giving the reader the full price, he leaves him hanging and transitions into the bonuses.

> I'll give you all the details on that in just a moment.
>
> But first, let me tell you about a few bonus gifts I'd like to send you for free today...

If you've paid close attention throughout, you'll see that I've used tons of open loops to tease the upcoming topics.

> I understand that some of these topics are difficult to understand through just the written word. And that's why I've set up a special bonus recording that walks you through each step of the sales letter. As the owner of this book, you can take advantage of this by visiting: www.daneknightonbook.com/theforbiddensecretbonus/

HOW TO GET GOOD AT COPYWRITING

1. Read killer copy every day (subscribe to the newsletters with the best copywriters).

2. Try to come up with a Big Idea every day.

3. Write copy every day.

I didn't say read all the copywriting books you can find. No! No! I'm also not saying you shouldn't read them at all; just don't spend all your time on them. Once you have a basic understanding, you really want to read copy—not read about copy. By doing this, you'll see patterns and trends emerge that you've never seen before. At first, it's like the matrix. But, once you know what to look for, it will pop right at you. Oh, and to state the obvious... you must put the reps in. You actually have to write.

THE FORBIDDEN SECRET

A s you and I are coming to a close here, I really want to take your hand and drill this point so deep into your skull that you never forget.

No matter how great the Big Idea, no matter how irresistible the offer, no matter how great the copy; if you break the prospect's already existing beliefs, your promotion is guaranteed to fail.

On the other hand, if you start with your prospect's model of the world and fit your claims into a logical sequence, matching their current story, feelings, and beliefs... and they agree with each new claim, you have accessed the hidden power of *The Forbidden Secret.*

Your job is to add one chain-link into another until you come full circle. Each chain-link represents a belief he must have before he will buy the product. If you can show him logically through every decision along the way, and he agrees to every step, you will have cracked the code to an undeniable sales argument.

First, you begin with the end in mind (the product or service), and then ask yourself all the statements and facts that your prospect already believes are true. The final product is the chain of logical reasoning. If you make just one claim that he doesn't believe, the entire chain will break and crumble.

Take a careful look at the image on the next page:

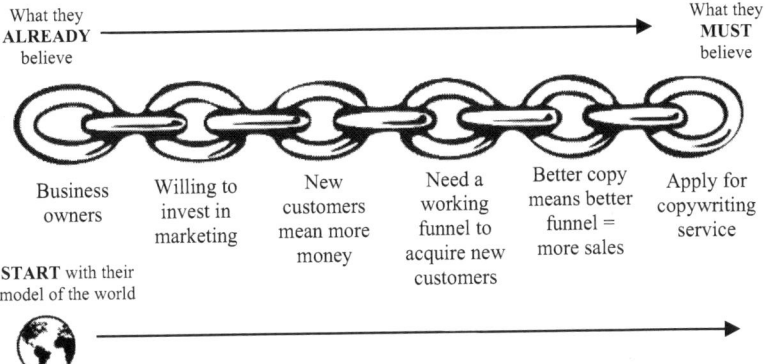

What they **ALREADY** believe

What they **MUST** believe

Business owners

START with their model of the world

Willing to invest in marketing

New customers mean more money

Need a working funnel to acquire new customers

Better copy means better funnel = more sales

Apply for copywriting service

Now that you've had a careful look at the image above, you can read the next page at your own leisure.

CONCLUSION

P hew!

That's a lot to take in.

At this point, you're probably a little overwhelmed by all the information, and I totally understand that. These concepts didn't come overnight. If only it was that easy. It came from tons and tons of digging. Buying courses, books, and everything I could get my hands on. All these principles I've shared have been proven repeatedly to work in both my own copy, and other businesses. You can rest assured, knowing these are tried and true principles that have worked in many different markets.

And that's why it's a good idea to refer to this book again and again. Think of it as a playbook rather than a one-time read. Every time you go to write a sales message, or check the copywriter that has written your sales message, run through this book and see if the main principles have been applied.

"There is no business problem, or 'any' problem for that matter, that cannot be solved with a great sales letter". — Gary Halbert

That is the power of copy. Your funnels, your ads, your landing page, your marketing… is nothing without great copy. Copy is the lifeblood of your business.

I have spent a great deal of time and effort to get this book in your hands. As you can imagine once this book is available to the public, I know it's going to be much harder to accommodate everyone who wants more personalized help.

That's why I bit my tongue and created something special for the readers of this book. That said, I can't make any promises this offer will still be available. As you may know, I have a rule where I only work with a handful of private clients at one time. Not everyone will be accepted when they go through the application process. Talking about the application process, here's how it works:

After you apply, my assistant will go through all the applications and select the best ones that fit the criteria. If you're successful, my assistant will get in contact with you to arrange a call. On the call, he'll find out more about your business, so that he can see if you're a good fit. If you are, then you might be speaking to me very shortly.

If you'd like the opportunity to work with me, then I suggest you apply here:

www.daneknightonbook.com/apply/

With that said...

It's time to close the curtains.

Dane Knighton

REFERENCES

Financial, Agora. *Newsletters and publications:* https://agorafinancial. com/

Brown, Todd. *Prospect Awareness Pyramid (image)* https:// themfanation.com/lesson-3-leadtypes

Warren, Blair. *Forbidden Keys to Persuasion*

Masterson Michael & Forde, John. *Great Leads: The 6 Easiest Ways to Start a Sales Message*

Bly, Bob. *The Copywriters Handbook*

Makepeace, Clayton. Google: *"The 20-point copywriting outline Clayton Makepeace"*

Gordon, David. *Phoenix: Therapeutic Patterns of Milton Erickson*

Schrieffer, Joe. *Agora Financial: Copy Boarding*

Sweets, Paleo. *Example image of frequently asked questions (FAQ)* https://www.mypaleorecipe.com/sweetsdev1?stick=1

Mauborgne, Renee and Kim Chan W. *Blue Ocean Strategy*

Bencivenga, Gary. *Bullet example:* http://marketingbullets.com/
available-on-dvds-for-the-first-and-only-time/

Green Juice, Organifi. *Image examples:* https://www.organifi.com/
green-juice/

Printed in Poland
by Amazon Fulfillment
Poland Sp. z o.o., Wrocław

54106413R00108